THE LITTLE BOOK OF RECURSION

HUW COLLINGBOURNE

bitwise books

The Little Book Of Recursion

ISBN: 978-1-913132-05-7

bitwise books is an imprint of **dark neon**

written by
Huw Collingbourne

DOWNLOAD THE SOURCE CODE

All the source code of the examples in this book may be downloaded (free) from the publisher's web site:
http://www.bitwisebooks.com/

Contents

Introduction

This book is all about recursion: a recursive function is one that calls itself instead of calling some other function. Recursion is an important programming technique. Let's see what you need to know before you begin studying this book.

Recursion is a powerful programming technique. This book explains what recursion is and how it works. The examples are mainly provided in the C and Ruby languages. However, you don't need to be a C or Ruby programmer in order to learn recursion from this book. The same recursive techniques can be used in all mainstream programming languages.

What is Recursion?

The word 'recursion' comes from Latin and it literally means to 'run back' or 'return'. In mathematics and programming, recursion means the repeated application of a rule or procedure. In this book, I use 'recursion' to describe the process of solving some problem by calling a function from within that same function. For example, if a function called `x()` contains some code that calls the `x()` function then I will refer to this as a 'recursive function-call'.

Download The Source Code

I recommend that you download the source code archive containing all the programs described in this book. The archive is available for free download from:

http://www.bitwisebooks.com/

This source code archive contains examples written in C, C# and Ruby. The C and C# programs are provided as Visual Studio solutions which may be loaded and run into Microsoft Visual Studio. If you are using some other C editor or IDE, you can also edit and run the examples simply by importing the source code files. The Ruby programs may be loaded into any Ruby editor or run from the command prompt using a Ruby interpreter.

Who Should Read This Book?

This book is suitable for intermediate and advanced programmers who need to understand how recursion works and the potential problems that may arise when doing recursive programming. It is not suitable for beginner programmers. I assume that you are already comfortable writing code in at least one programming language before you study this book.

Making Sense of the Text

In this book, any source code is written like this:

```
int add(int num1, int num2) {
    num1 = num1 + num2;
    return num1;
}
```

Any output that you may expect to see on screen when a program is run is shown like this:

```
The result of that calculation is 24!
```

When there is a sample program to accompany the code, the program name is shown above the code like this:

HelloWorld

```
// program code shown here
```

↵

When line of code is too long to fit onto the width of the page, I may have to break the line and put some of the code onto the next line. When a line-break has been added for formatting purposes, the break is shown by this character: ↵

Explanatory notes (which generally provide some hints or give a more in-depth explanation of some point mentioned in the text) are shown in a box like this:

Important

This is an explanatory note. You can skip it if you like – but if you do so, you may miss something of interest!

About the Author

Huw Collingbourne has been a programmer for more than 30 years. He is an online programming instructor with successful courses on C, C#, Java, Object Pascal, Ruby, JavaScript and other topics. For a full list of available courses be sure to visit the Bitwise Courses web site: http://bitwisecourses.com/

He is author of *The Little Book Of C* and *The Little Book Of Pointers* from Bitwise Books and *The Book Of Ruby* from No Starch Press. He is a well-known technology writer in the UK and has written numerous opinion and programming columns for a number of computer magazines, such as Computer Shopper, PC Pro, and PC Plus.

At various times Huw has been a magazine publisher, editor, and TV broadcaster. He has an MA in English from the University of Cambridge and holds a 2nd dan black belt in aikido, a martial art which he teaches in North Devon, UK. The aikido comes in useful when trying to keep his Pyrenean Mountain Dogs under some semblance of control.

About the Technical Editor

Dr. Dermot Hogan is a software developer who has led major projects written in Assembly Language, C , C# and a number of other programming languages. A specialist in real time trading technologies, he has managed and developed global risk management systems for several international banks and financial institutions. He is the lead developer of the independent software company, SapphireSteel Software. He holds a Ph.D in physics from the University of Cambridge. His current area of research is devoted to robotic control and imaging systems.

1 – Getting Started

How should you study this book? In the chapter I explain the assumptions I make about your programming experience and which software you need to get started.

This book is about the technique of recursion: what it is, how it works and why it is useful. You can, if you wish, follow the book just by reading the text. However, you will gain a much deeper understanding of recursion if you also download and run the sample projects from the source code archive. As most of these examples are supplied in the C and Ruby languages, you should ensure that you have installed a C compiler and Ruby interpreter for your operating system.

You will also need editors or IDEs (Integrated Development Environment) that support the C and Ruby syntax. But does that also mean that you need to be an expert C and Ruby programmer? No. The techniques described in this book can be used with all mainstream programming languages.

Which Languages Does the Book Apply To?

While most of the examples in the book are written in the C or Ruby languages, it is important to understand that you do not need to be a Ruby, or C programmer in order to follow this book. The code is intended to illustrate how recursion works. C and Ruby were chosen because a) the syntax of C will be familiar to many programmers who use languages such as C, C#, C++ or Java; and b) the Ruby syntax may be more accessible to people used to languages such as Ruby, Python and Pascal.

Once you understand the techniques described in this book, you will be able to apply them to whichever programming language you wish. In fact, it would be a good exercise to try 'translating' my sample code into some other language. The samples are deliberately short and simple to make them as easy as possible to understand.

How to Study This Book

In this book I provide lots of code samples to show how recursion works. But the best way to understand recursion is write your own code. If possible, I suggest that you use an IDE with a visual debugger so that you can step through the code to examine, line by line, what happens during recursion. Using a debugger to monitor the changing values of variables and watch how functions are called repeatedly (in the 'call stack') will help you to see what is happening in the process of recursion.

Do you need to read everything?

If you have never used recursion, you will get the most from this book by reading every chapter in order. If you are a more experienced programmer, feel free to jump into whichever chapters are of most interest to you. However, bear in mind that you must be sure that you fully understand what stack frames are and how they related to function-calls. If you don't have a solid understanding of the stack, you will never fully understand recursion. So don't skip Chapters 2 to 5, which explain stack frames and function-calls.

Editors and IDEs

In order to write C code you will need a C editor or IDE (Integrated Development Environment) and a C compiler. To write and run Ruby code will need a Ruby editor and interpreter. If you are unfamiliar with Ruby or C, you may find it easiest to install an IDE which includes all the other tools (compiler, interpreter, libraries etc.) to get you up and running as quickly as possible. You will find links to some free Ruby and C editors and tools in the Appendix of this book.

Understanding Ruby and C

This book does not go to any lengths to explain the details of the Ruby and C languages. The author (Huw Collingbourne) has written other books that teach how to program in Ruby and C. You can find links to additional learning resources in the Appendix.

What is Recursion For?

Some computer science books make it seem that recursion is an obscure technique whose only real use is for solving puzzles such as making neat piles of disks (the Tower of Hanoi) or plotting the movements of a knight around a chess board – (the Knight's Tour).

In this book, I'm not going to spend much time on puzzles. There are, in any case, hundreds of explanations of these types of puzzle in books and online so there is no point in going over them yet again. I will concentrate on more 'real world' situations in which recursion is needed to solve genuine programming problems.

So where, apart from puzzle-solving, is recursion used? As a matter of fact, it pops up in all sorts of unexpected places. If you are doing graphics operations, you may need to calculate complex shapes – such as fractals – recursively.

If you are doing natural language processing, or writing an interpreter capable of analysing mathematical expressions, it may be useful to do so with recursion. If you are writing a route-finder to calculate the optimal path between two points on a map, again recursion would be a useful technique.

In complex applications, recursion is used to traverse 'branching' structures. Fractal graphics, road maps, human language and programming language grammars can all be represented as branching structures. And that is why recursion is so useful.

Most of the examples I show in this book are kept deliberately simple. That's because I want you to gain a solid understanding of how recursion works. The examples at the beginning of the book are very simple indeed. Later in the book, we'll look at some more challenging programs including navigating through some tree-like structures such as the directories and subdirectories on a disk.

2 – Functions

Before you can understand how a *recursive* function-call works, you need to be sure that you understand how *any* function-call works. That's what this chapter is about.

In programming, a recursive function is one that calls itself. Here is an extremely simple recursive function written in C:

SimpleRecursion

```
void sum_recursion(int n) {
    printf("n is %d\n", n);
    n += 1;
    if (n < 3) {
        sum_recursion(n);
    }
}
```

The `sum_recursion()` function prints the value of the `int` parameter `n`, then adds 1 to `n` and calls itself with this new value. The function stops calling itself when the value of `n` is 3 or more. This is how I call the function at the outset:

```
int main() {
    sum_recursion(0);
}
```

So initially, `n` is 0 and the `printf()` statement displays that value. The `sum_recursion()` function adds 1 to `n` (`n += 1`) and calls itself with this value (`sum_recursion(n)`). The new value of `n (1)`, is displayed by the `printf()` statement. And once again 1 is added to `n`. `sum_recursion()` is called with the new value (`2`). This is displayed. Again 1 is added to `n`. At this point `n` has the value 3, so the test in the `while` loop fails because `n` is no longer less than 3:

```
if (n < 3)
```

This is the output produced by this program:

```
n is 0
n is 1
n is 2
```

So here I've written a recursive function that can count from 0 to 2. Admittedly, that is not a very useful thing to do. There are easier ways to count numbers. Nevertheless, it illustrates the fundamentals of how recursion works. All the examples given in this book essentially work in the same way as this simple function even though some of them may look a lot more complicated.

What is a Function?

Maybe you think of a function as a convenient way of dividing up long programs into shorter pieces. But there is much more to a function than that. Here I want to make sure that you understand exactly how a function works when it is executed by the computer.

Writing a Function

When you *write* a function, you write code in a named block which can be called, by name, from other bits of code.

Executing a Function

Bu when a function is *executed*, by the computer, a block of memory (a 'stack frame') is set aside for it to run in. And *that* is what we really need to focus on.

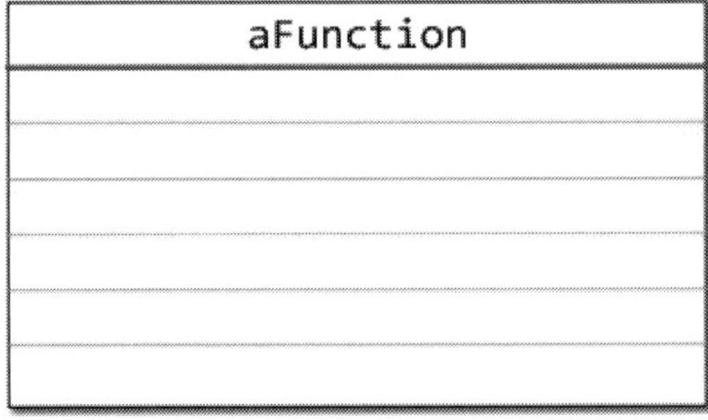

The block of memory set aside for a function contains any local variables within that function. When two functions are called, two different blocks of memory are set aside, each containing different sets of local variables.

aFunction
variable1
variable2
variable3

anotherFunction
variable1
variable2
variable3

You could imagine functions as being like index cards. I have two index cards that I keep in my petty cash box. I've given each card a name: *Index Card 1* is called "Pay Vet". *Index Card 2* is called "Pay Dentist". Those index cards represent two functions in my program: `pay_vet()` and `pay_dentist()`:

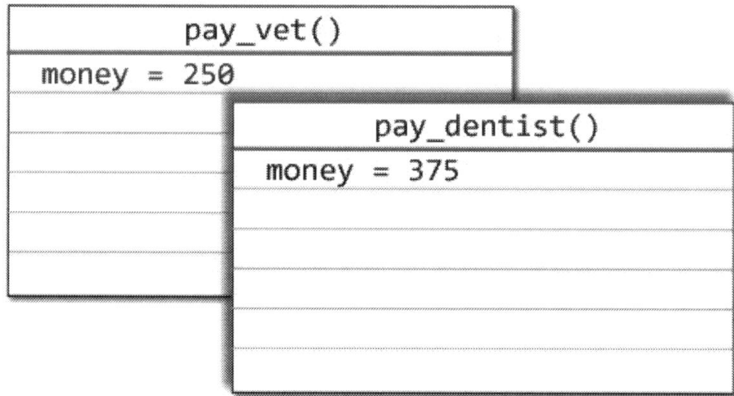

Each index card (or function) contains a value (or variable) labelled 'money'. Even though the name is the same, these represent different values on different index cards – or within different functions. Keep that idea in mind. It will be important later on.

What is a Function call?

When function `a()` calls function `b()`, a new chunk of memory is set aside for function `b()`. When function `b()` exits the program execution returns to the line of code inside function `a()` immediately after the line of code that called function `b()`.

In this illustration, `a()` calls `b()`. When b() returns, it is the line that I've called `some_more_code`, which immediately follows the function-call, that is run next:

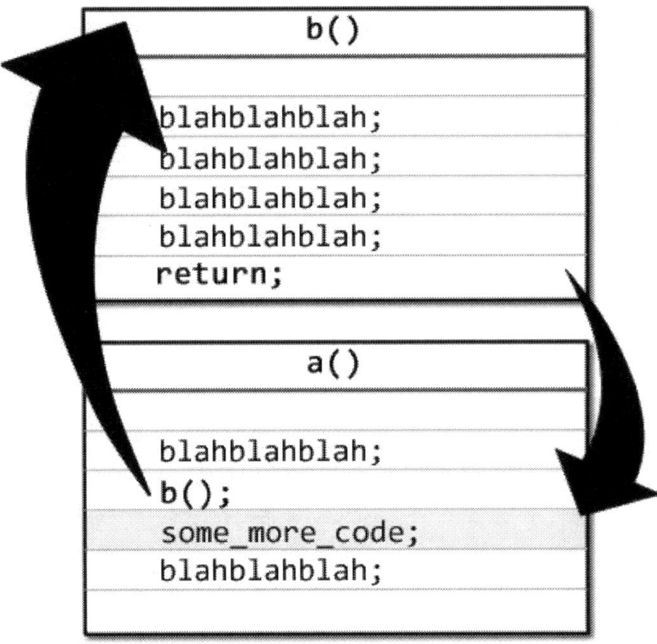

The same is true with recursive functions. If function `a()` calls *itself,* function `a()`, recursively, a new chunk of memory is set aside for a second copy of function `a()`. When the *second* copy of function `a()` exits, the program returns to the line of code inside the *first* copy of function `a()` immediately after the line that called function `a()` recursively.

What's in a Name?

As far as the computer is concerned, calling function `b()` from function `a()` isn't really much different from calling function `a()` from function `a()`. In both cases, when a function is called, a new chunk of memory is set aside for it.

Now look at the illustration below. At first sight, it might seem odd that I've shown two copies of the same function. That's because there really *are* two copies – not of the function's source code but of its *state*. Think of these as 'working copies' – areas in memory where the internal state of the function, such as the values of its local variables and parameters are stored while the function is running. Here these two working copies are two stack frames. Two separate blocks of memory.

In order to understanding recursion, you have to stop thinking of a single function as *literally* calling itself. What it is really doing is calling *copies* of itself. If you find that idea hard to grasp at the moment, don't worry. I'll explain it in much more detail later in the book.

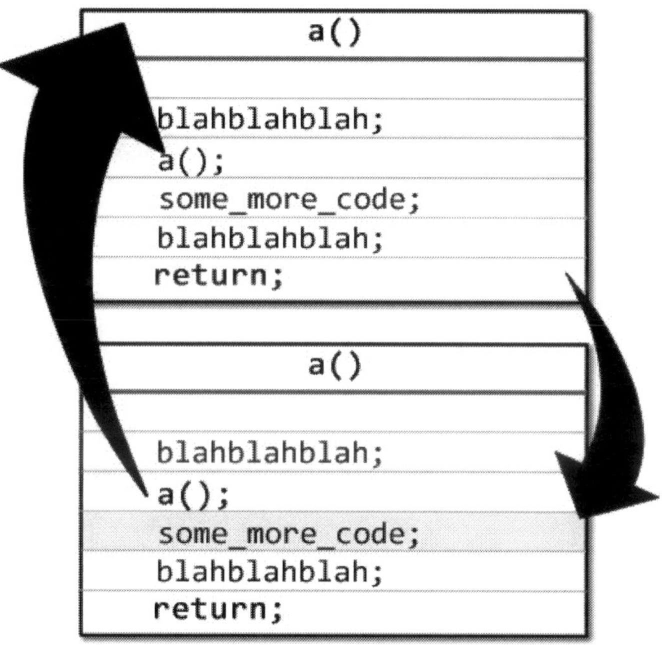

3 – Understanding Recursion

In this chapter I'll explain the fundamentals of recursion. Along the way, I'll also explain some important details of the computer architecture – how a computer actually works – which will be vital to a proper understanding of recursion.

You can write recursive functions in whichever language you happen to be using. In fact, it would be a good exercise to try to translate my examples into another language – Python, Java, Basic or Pascal, for example. In fact, I strongly recommend that you try to write our own recursive functions as you progress through the book. I will provide lots examples that you can use a basis for your own code.

A Simple Recursive Function

Let's begin by taking a look at a very short recursive function. This is similar (but not identical!) to the recursive function I showed in the last chapter. I've written this program both in C and in Ruby. Both versions work in exactly the same way. This is the Ruby code:

Recursion (Ruby)

```
$total = 0

def sum_recursion( n )
  n += 1
  $total +=1
  puts( "n is #{n}, $total is #{$total}" )
  if $total < 3 then
      sum_recursion( n )
  end
  puts( "...n is #{n}, $total is #{$total}" )
end

puts( "At START: $total is #{$total}" )
sum_recursion( 0 )
puts( "At END: $total is #{$total}" )
```

And this is the C code:

Recursion (C)

```
#include <stdio.h>

int total = 0;

void sum_recursion(int n) {
    n += 1;
    total += 1;
    printf("n is %d, total is %d\n", n, total);
    if (total < 3) {
        sum_recursion(n);
    }
    printf("...n is %d, total is %d\n", n, total);
}

int main(int argc, char **argv) {
    printf("At START: total is %d\n", total);
    sum_recursion(0);
    printf("At END: total is %d\n", total);
    return 0;
}
```

If you run the two programs, the output will be almost identical in both cases:

```
At START: total is 0
n is 1, total is 1
n is 2, total is 2
n is 3, total is 3
...n is 3, total is 3
...n is 2, total is 3
...n is 1, total is 3
At END: total is 3
```

Even though the code here is really short and simple, if you are new to recursion it may nevertheless be quite hard to understand exactly what's going on. For that reason, I am going to explain this short program in minute detail.

What does the code do?

As in the example from Chapter 2, the purpose of the `sum_recursion()` function is to count from 1 to 3. The function receives an integer argument which is assigned to the parameter, `n`. So `n` is scoped *inside* the `sum_recursion()` function. It is local to the function.

The code that calls the `sum_recursion()` function initially is in the 'main' scope (in C, it is in the `main()` function) and so it cannot access the value of `n`. But it *can* access the value of the global variable, `total` (or `$total` in Ruby), because that is scoped *outside* the function.

C, Ruby and Other Languages

Here I show fragments of code from C and Ruby programs. In fact, the syntax of the languages is unimportant. You could write recursive functions in other languages and they would work in much the same way.

Whenever the `sum_recursion()` function executes, 1 is added to `n` and 1 is also added to `total`. Then, just so long as `total` is less than 3, the code inside the `sum_recursion()` function calls the same function, `sum_recursion()`, passing to it the new value of `n`:

```
if (total < 3) {
    sum_recursion(n);
}
```

The process or recursion is started off in the 'main' scope by calling `sum_recursion()` with the value 0:

```
sum_recursion(0);
```

To understand what happens next I'm going to step through the program in a debugger.

Debuggers

In the screenshots that follow I use the Visual Studio debugger to step through the execution of a C program. While debuggers are usually provided in C and C++ IDEs, not all editors and IDEs for all languages have this capability. A good debugger will greatly assist your understanding of recursion. However, if you don't have a debugger, you may want to add *print* statements at crucial points in your code so that you can check how the values of variables change. For example, in my Ruby program I print the values of the variables `n` and `$total` like this:

```
puts( "n is #{n}, $total is #{$total}" )
```

Debugging Recursion

Here I am debugging the C *Recursion* project using Microsoft Visual Studio. You can, of course, also use other IDEs to debug programs written in C and other languages. The debugging options are not identical in all integrated debuggers. It is worth taking a little time to become familiar with your IDE's debugging capabilities. A good debugger will really help you to understand how recursion works.

Set Breakpoints

The first thing I do is place breakpoints that mark the places where the program will pause so that I can examine the values of variables at those points.

```
1   #include <stdio.h>
2
3   int total = 0;
4
5   void sum_recursion(int n) {
6       n += 1;
7       total += 1;
8       printf("n is %d, total is %d\n", n, total);
9       if (total < 3) {
10          sum_recursion(n);
11      }
12      printf("...n is %d, total is %d\n", n, total);
13  }
14
15
16  int main(int argc, char **argv) {
17      printf("At START: total is %d\n", total);
18      sum_recursion(0);
19      printf("At END: total is %d\n", total);
20      return 0;
21  }
```

I've placed one breakpoint on the recursive call to the `sum_recursion()` function on line 10. I've placed another breakpoint on the `printf()` statement on line 12. And I've added a third breakpoint right at the end of the program on line 20.

In Visual Studio, breakpoints are added by clicking in the margin of the editor and they are indicated by red circles in the margin.

Watch Variables

I've added the variables n and total to the Watch window. The Watch window shows the values of variables as they change during the execution of the program. I start the debugger (I press F5) and it breaks the first time sum_recursion() is called recursively.

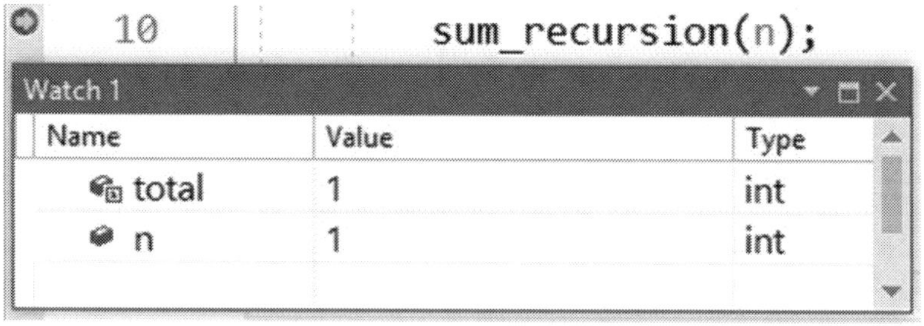

This code in sum_recursion() adds 1 to both n and total, so by the time the first breakpoint (on line 10) is hit in the first call to this function, both variables have the value 1. The test (total < 3) evaluates to true, so n (1) is now passed as an argument when the sum_recursion() function is called recursively:

```
if (total < 3) {
    sum_recursion(n);          // n is now 1
}
```

I continue in the debugger (F5) until the breakpoint on line 10 is hit again. Once again 1 is added to both variables, so n is now 2 and total is also 2.

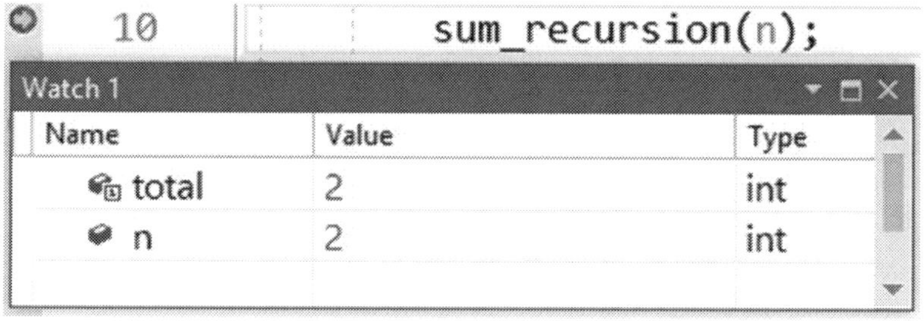

Now n (2) is once more passed to sum_recursion():

```
if (total < 3) {
    sum_recursion(n);          // n is now 2
}
```

I continue debugging (**F5**) and now the breakpoint on line 10 is again hit in the recursive function-call. Yet again 1 is added to both variables giving each the value 3.

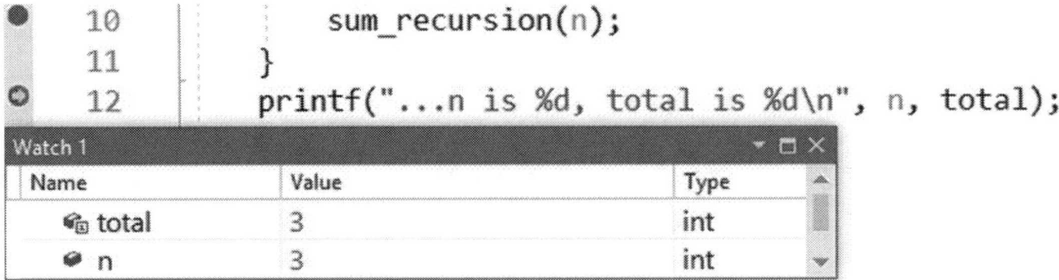

This time, however, the test condition `(total < 3)` fails because `total` is no longer less than 3. So the code that calls the function recursively, on line 10, is skipped – and the breakpoint on line 10 isn't hit. Instead the next line of code after the if block is executed, that's the `printf()` on line 12, and that breakpoint is hit.

Stepping Through Code

This time I decide to execute just one line of code (here that's the `printf()` statement where I've hit the breakpoint on line 12) by 'stepping into' it (**F10** in Visual Studio). Now `printf()` prints out the values of `n` and `total` which, as expected, are both 3.

```
...n is 3, total is 3
```

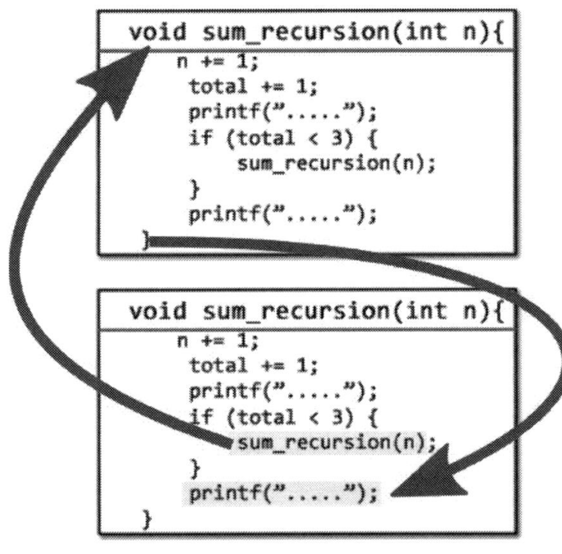

Having arrived at the end of this function, the 'flow of control' moves back to the line of code *immediately following the code that originally called the function*. Here, the code that called `sum_recursion()` happens to be inside the function itself. And the line of code that follows the function-call is the `printf()` statement on line 12.

So, remembering that each function-call creates a new 'copy' of the function in memory, you can think of `sum_recursion()#1` calling `sum_recursion()#2`.

When `sum_recursion()#2` exits, the next line of code in `sum_recursion()#1` (here that's the `printf()` on line 12) is run.

I keep pressing **F5** to carry on debugging and I keep landing on the breakpoint on line 12. As the function keeps calling itself recursively a whole 'stack' of executing functions is created. This stack keeps growing until the 'end condition' is met (here that's when `total` is no longer less than 3). At that point, the recursion 'unwinds'.

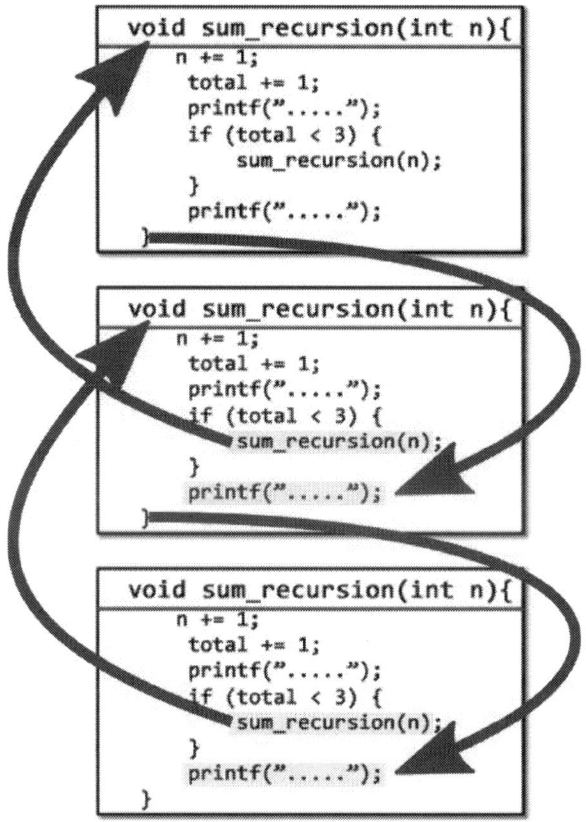

By 'unwinding', I mean that the function-call on the top of the stack exits and execution returns to the one before it. Then *that* exits and so on …

When I run this program, this is what I see:

```
...n is 3, total is 3
...n is 2, total is 3
...n is 1, total is 3
```

The value of the global variable, `total`, is unaffected by the 'unwinding' of the recursion. It retains its final value 3. But each time the `printf()` is hit on line 12, the value of the parameter, `n`, which is *local* to the function, has the value it had *before* the previous time we called `sum_recursion()` recursively.

That's because as the recursion unwinds we are going back 'down' the stack to each 'previous' function-call and so we have returned to a function in which the parameter, `n`, was one less than the function from which we just returned.

Look at the diagram on the previous page to understand this. Each function-call uses a separate chunk of memory. I show each chunk of memory as an index card. Each index card is separate from each other index card just as each chunk of memory is separate from every other chunk of memory.

Stack Frames and Local Variables

Each function-call's block of memory or 'stack frame' contains a separate 'copy' of any local variables or parameters such as `n`. We look at the call stack and stack frames in detail in Chapter 4.

As each function-call exits the program execution returns to the previous function-call. The value of any local variables or parameters in that context hasn't changed. You can think of each function-call as creating a block of memory to save the 'execution state' of that function.

The function, just like the index cards in my diagrams, has one name, `sum_recursion()`. But when that function is called three times, three separate blocks of memory are used. Here I append numbers to the function name to indicate three function-calls: `sum_recursion()#1`, `sum_recursion()#2` and `sum_recursion()#3`. At each function-call, the value of `n` is incremented (and stored in a separate block of memory), like this:

`n` was 1 in `sum_recursion()#1`
`n` was 2 in `sum_recursion()#2`
`n` was 3 in `sum_recursion()#3`

As we backtrack through those function-calls (as the recursion unwinds), `n` retains its values in each of those three blocks of memory:

`n` is 3 in `sum_recursion()#3`
`n` is 2 in `sum_recursion()#2`
`n` is 1 in `sum_recursion()#1`

Recursive function-calls are like 'normal' function-calls

If this seems confusing, just try to think what would have happened if `n` had been 2 in the `sum_recursion()` function and then we called some other, *unrelated*, function.

On returning from that unrelated function, `n` would, of course, still have the value 2 in the `sum_recursion()` function. That's all that's happened here. The only difference is that *this* function happens to call *itself* rather than some *other* function. But when it returns from that recursive function-call, the values of its local variables are unaffected – just as they would be if a different function-call had been made.

The `total` variable, however, lives *outside* the function and is unaffected by recursion so, while the value of `n` changes during the unwinding of recursion, the value of the global variable, `total`, retains its final value 3.

Recursion and variable scope

Let's take a bit more time to be absolutely clear about how local variables are affected by recursion.

I've rewritten the *Recursion* project – the one we just looked at in C – with some more printed output in the *Recursion1* project. I've also added a local variable `callnum` to show which *level* of recursion we are in at any time.

Recursion1

```
int total = 0;

void sum_recursion(int callnum, int n) {
    int localtotal;

    callnum++;
    if (callnum <= 3) {
        localtotal = n + 1;
        total = n + 1;
        printf("a) In sum_recursion() call#%d localtotal=%d, total=%d\n",
            callnum, localtotal, total);
        sum_recursion(callnum, localtotal);
        printf("b) In sum_recursion() call#%d localtotal=%d, total=%d\n",
            callnum, localtotal, total);
    }
}
```

If you want to run this program in a debugger, put a breakpoint on line 24 (the last code line of `main()`), then step through the recursive calls. You will see that both the local variable `localtotal` and the global variable `total` are incremented: 1 then 2, then 3.

```
a) In sum_recursion() call#1 localtotal=1, total=1
a) In sum_recursion() call#2 localtotal=2, total=2
a) In sum_recursion() call#3 localtotal=3, total=3
```

But as the recursion *unwinds* – that is, as the code execution goes back down through the stack of function-calls – the value of `localtotal` remains *as it was* in the scope of each function-call. But the global variable, `total`, which was declared outside the scope of the function, retains its *final value*. It doesn't change when the recursion unwinds.

```
b) In sum_recursion() call#3 localtotal=3, total=3
b) In sum_recursion() call#2 localtotal=2, total=3
b) In sum_recursion() call#1 localtotal=1, total=3
```

4 – The Call Stack

When you call a function, a block of memory called a stack frame is added to a structure called the stack. In order to understand recursion, it is vital to understand the stack. That is what this chapter is about.

In previous chapters, I've represented functions as index cards. Each card represents a separate block of memory – a working area for the function.

When functions call other functions – or, when one function calls itself – you end up with a stack of memory-blocks that you can imagine as being a bit like a stack of index cards. Now let's find out what that stack really is.

Stack Frames

If you program an object oriented language, you will no doubt be familiar with the idea that each object wraps up its internal state (including its local variables) in its own block of memory. In most object oriented languages, the definition of an object is written in a class. When an actual, usable object, is created from that definition, we can say that the object is an 'instance' of its class.

Function-calls are a bit like that. Each function-call, in effect creates an 'instance' of the function. I don't mean that it has anything to do with object orientation. It hasn't. But, just as an object is an instance of a class definition, a working function is a sort of 'instance' of a function definition. It is wrapped up inside its own little chunk of memory with its own internal 'state' (its local variables and parameters). But instead of talking about the *instance* of a function, it is more correct to talk about a *frame* on the *stack*.

The stack is the area of computer memory reserved for temporary values such as a function's local variables which come into existence and go out of existence as functions are called and then return. That's why the blocks of working memory for functions are called *stack frames*. Call a function and a new 'frame' is put onto the 'stack'.

Debugging the Call Stack

A debugger that can show the call stack may help you understand how stack frames are put onto the stack and taken off again.

The stack is a last-in, first out (LIFO) structure. That means that it is built up by putting frames one on top of the other. And when frames are removed from the stack, the last one that was added to it is the first one to be removed.

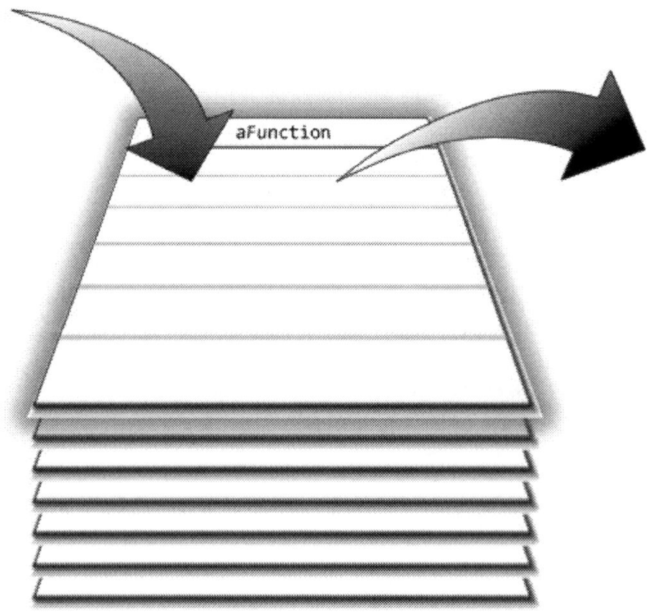

Let's see this in a debugger. Here I will use the Visual Studio debugger once again to step through the *Recursion* project, with breakpoints set on lines 10, 12 and 20. When I did this before, I was mainly interested in keeping track of the values of variables. This time I am going to concentrate on the Call Stack. To view the Call Stack in Visual Studio you need to start a debugging session (F5) and make sure the Call Stack Window is shown (select the *Debug* menu, *Windows*, *Call Stack*). The debugger hits the breakpoint on line 10. This is what I see in the Call Stack.

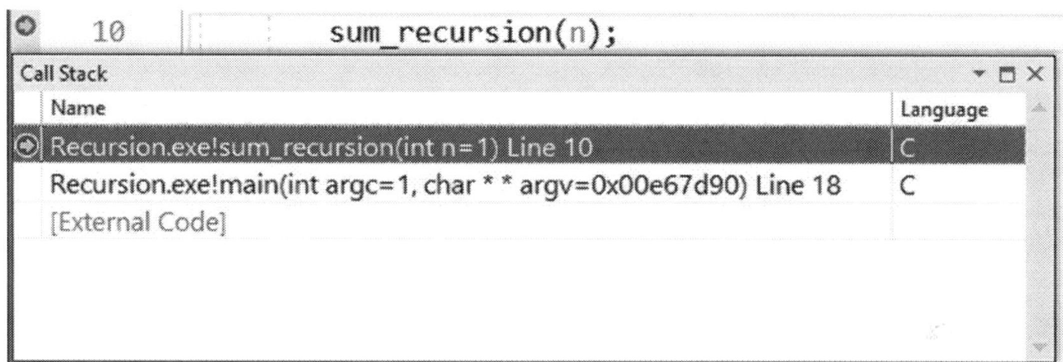

This shows that the `main()` function in *Recursion.exe* has executed (this is the bottom line in the Call Stack window and the bottom 'frame' in the stack) but I am currently in the `sum_recursion()`function (the highlighted line which is at the top of the stack) and the value of `n` is 1.

I press F5 to continue debugging. Now I am in `sum_recursion()` again. But this time there are two entries for `sum_recursion()`. The one top of the stack is highlighted (here `n` is 2) and this is a recursive call from the one beneath it (where `n` is still 1).

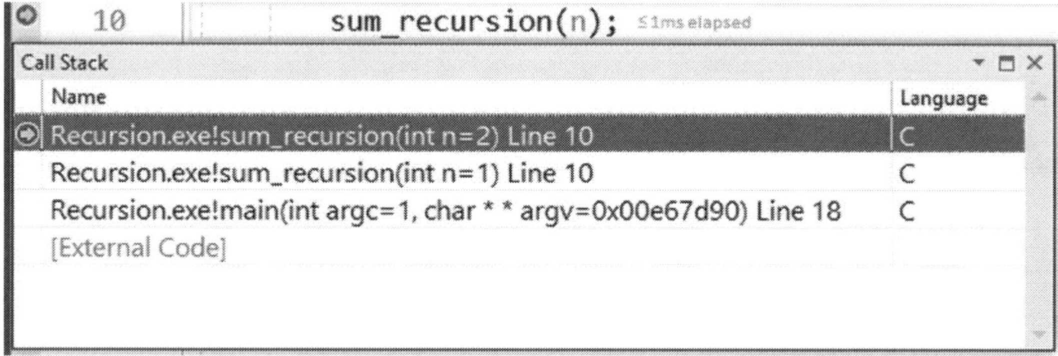

I continue debugging (F5). There is another call to `sum_recursion()`. Another frame is put onto the stack. But this time the value of the global variable `total` (and also of the parameter `n`) is 3, so the test `(total < 3)` fails. That means the breakpoint on line 10 is skipped and we hit the breakpoint on line 12.

```
12        printf("...n is %d, total is %d\n", n, total);
```

Call Stack	
Name	Language
Recursion.exe!sum_recursion(int n=3) Line 12	C
Recursion.exe!sum_recursion(int n=2) Line 10	C
Recursion.exe!sum_recursion(int n=1) Line 10	C
Recursion.exe!main(int argc=1, char * * argv=0x00e67d90) Line 18	C
[External Code]	

Here we can see that the `main()` function executes – that's the bottom line in the Call Stack window. The `main()` function calls `sum_recursion()` (the next line up in the Call Stack window) where `n` equals 1. A recursive call is then made to `sum_recursion()` where `n` equals 2. Then another recursive call is made to `sum_recursion()` where `n` equals 3 (that's shown on the top line which is highlighted).

Now if I carry on debugging, I can see that, as each function exits, a frame is taken (or 'popped') off the stack. Here, for instance, since there is no more code to be run in the third call to `sum_recursion()` that function (that is, the third 'working copy' of the function) exits.

No more memory is needed to store its state so its frame is removed from the stack as you can see here:

```
12        printf("...n is %d, total is %d\n", n, total);
```

Call Stack	
Name	Language
Recursion.exe!sum_recursion(int n=2) Line 12	C
Recursion.exe!sum_recursion(int n=1) Line 10	C
Recursion.exe!main(int argc=1, char * * argv=0x00e67d90) Line 18	C
[External Code]	

If I carry on debugging I will see the other frames being taken off the stack until finally I return to the frame of the `main()` function.

Pushing and Popping

The usual jargon terms for adding and removing items from a stack are 'pushing' and 'popping'. An item is pushed (added) to the top of the stack and popped (removed) from the stack.

The Call Stack and Variables

If you are using a debugger you may want to keep open a Watch window to examine the values of variables at each successive call of a function. Here I am debugging the *Recursion1* project and I have hit the third call to the `sum_recursion()` function:

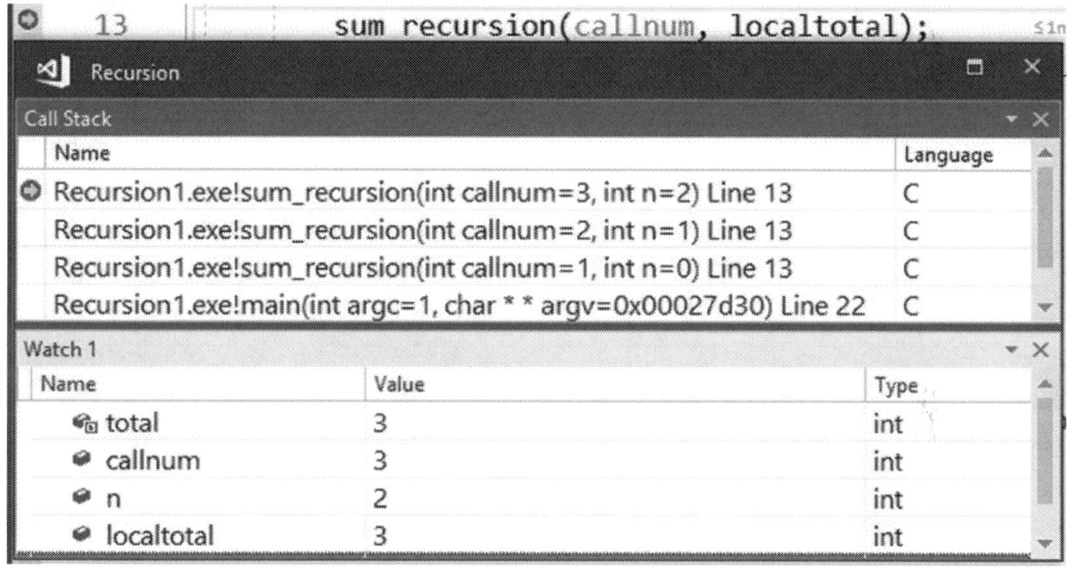

Pay attention to the values of the two `int` parameters, `callnum` and `n` and also the variable `localtotal`, all of which are *local* to this function whereas `total` is declared outside the function and has global scope.

Using the Visual Studio Call Stack window I can double-click on specific frames (the highlighted line) to navigate through the stack and see the values of variables in each selected frame.

As I navigate 'back' through the Call Stack, the values of the *local* variables and parameters change but the *global* variable stays the same:

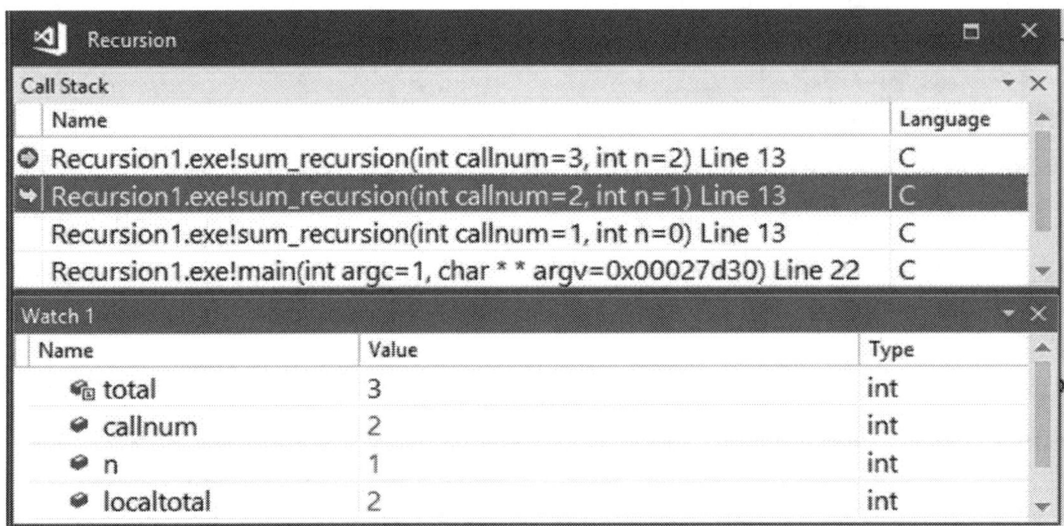

This shows quite clearly that the local variables (and parameters) are isolated from one another in each function-call – in each 'frame' on the stack.

Even though I've called the same function recursively, I have separate copies of the local variables each time it is called.

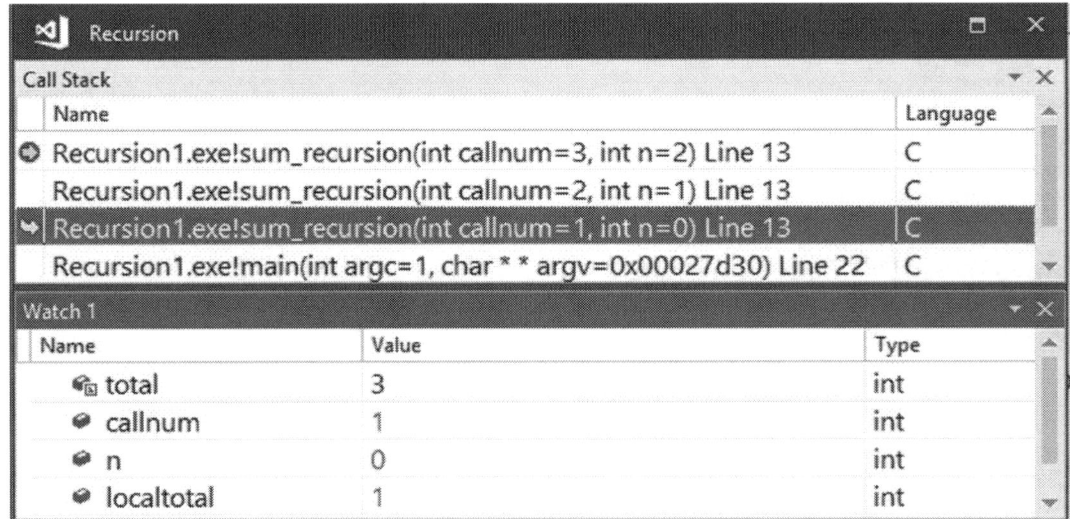

Recursive Calculations

Up to now my recursive functions have just counted up to 3 which (I would have to admit!) is not an amazingly interesting or useful thing to do. The code in the *Recursion2* project is only slightly more complicated than the projects that we looked at previously. But it is a bit more interesting. It calculates the sum of a series of natural numbers:

Recursion2

```
#include <stdio.h>

int total = 0;

void sum_recursion(int callnum, int n) {
    int newnum;

    callnum++;
    printf("Enter\t\t#[%d]: sum_recursion(n=%d)\n", callnum, n);
    if (n > 0) {
        newnum = n - 1;
        total = n + total;
        printf("  before\t#[%d]: sum_recursion(%d)\n", callnum, newnum);
        sum_recursion(callnum, newnum);
        printf("  after \t#[%d]: total=%d\n", callnum, total);
    }
    printf("Return: n=%d, total=%d\n", n, total);
}

int main(int argc, char **argv) {
    int startnum = 3;

    sum_recursion(0, startnum);
    printf("\nmain: Sum of the first %d integers using recursion is %d\n",
         startnum, total);
    return 0;
}
```

If I call `sum_recursion()` with 3, it calculates the total of adding 1, 2 and 3 and returns 6. If I call it with 4, It calculates 1+2+3+4 and returns 10. To do this it subtracts 1 from the argument `n`, assigns the new value to the local variable `newnum` and calls itself recursively with that value. The value of `total` is calculated by adding the values of `n`:

```
newnum = n - 1;
total = n + total;
sum_recursion(callnum, newnum);
```

Once again, I've also added a `callnum` argument which calculates the number of times the function has been called. There are some `printf()` statements to print the values of `n`, `newnum` and `callnum`, to help you to understand what is happening by studying the output.

At first sight, this function may seem a bit more complicated than the last one, because of the calculation involved. But in terms of how the recursion works, it really isn't more complicated at all. This is what is shown when the program runs:

```
Enter               #[1]: sum_recursion(n=3)
  before            #[1]: sum_recursion(2)
Enter               #[2]: sum_recursion(n=2)
  before            #[2]: sum_recursion(1)
Enter               #[3]: sum_recursion(n=1)
  before            #[3]: sum_recursion(0)
Enter               #[4]: sum_recursion(n=0)
Return: n=0, total=0
  after             #[3]: total=1
Return: n=1, total=1
  after             #[2]: total=3
Return: n=2, total=3
  after             #[1]: total=6
Return: n=3, total=6

main: Sum of the first 3 integers using recursion is 6
```

You can see that the value of `n` is decremented with each function-call: 3, 2, 1.

```
Enter               #[1]: sum_recursion(n=3)
Enter               #[2]: sum_recursion(n=2)
Enter               #[3]: sum_recursion(n=1)
Enter               #[4]: sum_recursion(n=0)
```

As the recursion unwinds, we backtrack through those function-calls and we see the value of `n` local to each function-call: 0, then 1, then 2, then 3. The value of `total`, which is declared outside the function, remains at its *final* calculated value and is unaffected by the unwinding of the recursion. It's final value is 6 and that's how it stays.

Let's be clear about this: when each function-call exits (that is, when it returns control to the previous function-call or stack frame), the value of `n` is 'lost'. The value of `n` is local to each stack frame and when that frame exits, that local value vanishes.

But the value of `total` (which is declared outside the function) is not affected when a stack frame is removed. In this example, the final calculated value of `n` was 1 but that value is 'lost' as recursion unwinds and we return to an 'earlier' value of `n` – until that value too is lost when execution returns to `main()`. But the final calculated value of `total` was 6 and that value is retained:

```
Return: n=0, total=6
Return: n=1, total=6
Return: n=2, total=6
```

You must be sure to initialize the global variable `total` with a starting value. This can be done in the `main()` function or, as I did, it can be initialized at the time of its declaration:

```
int total = 0;
```

Incidentally, the code of `sum_recursion()` is somewhat complicated by the use of the `callnum` and `newnum` variables and all the `printf()` statements used to display the values of variables. For that reason, I have also included a simplified version of the function called `sum_recursion_simplified()`. This has exactly the same code logic as the `sum_recursion()` function and you may find is easier to understand:

```
void sum_recursion_simplified(int callnum, int n) {
    if (n > 0) {
        sum_recursion_simplified(callnum, n - 1);
        total += n;
    }
}
```

Using global variables to store values works fine. But since it is generally better programming practice to avoid globals whenever possible, let's see how we can accumulate a total in a different way – using the values returned by each recursively-called function. That is the subject of the next chapter.

Call Stack Navigation

Each line in the Call Stack window represents one 'frame' of the stack. A frame is a block of memory that contains the internal 'state' of a function that has been called. This includes (among other things) the values of variables and parameters that are local to that function. When I use a Call Stack window to 'navigate' the stack, I can move from one 'frame' to another and take a look at its internal state – here, the values of the local variables and parameters.

5 – Return Values

How does a function that calls itself return a value to itself? This may sound more complicated than it really is …

In this chapter, we'll take a look at the *Recursion3* project. This is essentially the same as *Recursion2* which we looked at in Chapter 4. Once again, the `sum_recursion()` function calculates a series of numbers:

Recursion3

```
int sum_recursion(int callnum, int n) {
    int total;
    int newnum;

    callnum++;
    printf("Enter\t\t#[%d]: sum_recursion(n=%d)\n", callnum, n);
    if (n == 1) {
        total = 1;
        printf("End condition met! total=%d\n", total);
    } else {
        newnum = n - 1;
        printf("  before\t#[%d]: sum_recursion(%d)\n", callnum, newnum);
        total = n + sum_recursion(callnum, newnum);
        printf("  after \t#[%d]: total=%d\n", callnum, total);
    }
    printf("Return: n=%d, total=%d\n", n, total);
    return total;
}
```

But there's a difference. I no longer use a *global* variable `total` (declared outside the function), to store the calculated value. You may recall that in *Recursion2* I initialized the global variable at the time of its declaration:

```
int total = 0;
```

In the *Recursion3* project, I don't use a global variable to store the value of `total`. Instead, the function has a local variable called `total` whose value is returned by the function:

```
return total;
```

When the function has been called recursively, that returned value is passed back to the code that called the function which happens to be this:

```
total = n + sum_recursion(callnum, newnum);
```

So each time the `sum_recursion()` function exits, the value that it returns is added to the value of `n` within the scope of the currently executing function (that is, the current stack frame) and this value is assigned to `total`.

Incidentally, since `total` is now a local variable, I cannot initialize its value before calling `sum_recursion()`. Instead, I have to initialize the 'starting' value of `total` within the function itself. I do that when the end condition of the recursion has been met (here that is when `n` has the value 1). At this point, I assign the value 1 to `total`:

```
if (n == 1) {
    total = 1;
    printf("End condition met! total=%d\n", total);
}
```

This is the output:

```
Enter           #[1]: sum_recursion(n=3)
  before        #[1]: sum_recursion(2)
Enter           #[2]: sum_recursion(n=2)
  before        #[2]: sum_recursion(1)
Enter           #[3]: sum_recursion(n=1)
     --- End condition met! total=1 ---
Return: n=1, total=1
  after         #[2]: total=3
Return: n=2, total=3
  after         #[1]: total=6
Return: n=3, total=6

main: Sum of the first 3 integers using recursion is 6
```

If you haven't used returned values in recursion before it may take a while to get used to recursive functions that return values. I'm going to look at returned values in more detail shortly. But first, let me take a brief look at the *Recursion3* program translated into another programming language – Ruby.

Recursion in Ruby

Recursive functions work just the same way in other programming languages as they do in C. Here I've translated the C project, *Recursion3*, into Ruby.

Recursion3 (Ruby)

```
def sumRecursion( callnum, n )
  callnum += 1
  puts( "Enter \t\t#[#{callnum}]: SumRecursion(n=#{n})" )
  if n == 1 then
    total = 1
    puts( "     --- End condition met! total=#{total} ---" )
  else
    newnum = n - 1
    puts( "  before\t#[#{callnum}]: SumRecursion(#{newnum})" )
    total = n + sumRecursion( callnum, newnum )
    puts( "  after\t\t#[#{callnum}]: total=#{total}" )
  end
  puts( "Return: n=#{n}, total= #{total}" )
  return total
end

startnum = 3
puts( "\nSum of the first #{startnum} integers using recursion is")
puts( "#{sumRecursion( 0, startnum )}" )
```

C and Ruby are very different languages. C is compiled, Ruby is interpreted. Ruby is Object Oriented, C isn't. C requires variables to be pre-declared with their types and it also requires that functions declare their return types. Ruby doesn't require this typing information for either variables or functions.

Moreover, as you can see, the syntax of the two languages could hardly be more different. Even so, when I run the C program and I run the Ruby program, the output is identical.

If you are familiar with Ruby, you will realise that some of the syntax I've used here is not strictly necessary. I don't even need all the parentheses, nor do I need the `return` keyword at the end of the function. But I've tried to make this as close as possible to the C code so that anyone who doesn't know Ruby will be able to follow the program more easily. Or you might even want to translate the Ruby code into the syntax of some other programming language.

As in the C version of this program, the big change from previous examples is the way the code makes use of the value returned from the function. So how does this actually work?

In this project the accumulated total is no longer assigned to a variable declared *outside* the scope of the function. Instead, the `sum_recursion()` function – in both the C and Ruby versions of the code – returns the value of the *local* variable `total`, which is an integer. After each recursive function-call that value, `total`, is recalculated as `n` plus the return value of `sum_recursion()`:

```
total = n + sum_recursion(callnum, newnum)
```

But why, you may wonder, doesn't the value of `total` get lost when the recursion unwinds? I said earlier that the values of local variables are discarded when a function exits. However, it turns out that return values are special.

Return values are special

In the *Recursion3* project, we have a function, `sum_recursion()`, which returns an integer value. That value is calculated inside the function and it is assigned to the local variable, `total`. It is the value of `total` that is returned. That returned value is then used by the code that called the function recursively.

But how can that be? We know that the stack frame – the memory that stores local variables when a function runs – is discarded when the function exits. At that point the values of the local variables are lost. However, this is not true for return values. These are treated specially. That's true, incidentally, for the values returned from *all* functions, whether or not they happen to be called recursively.

All Returns are Special!

Don't get bogged down with the idea of returning local variable values recursively. It is not very useful to try to imagine the process of assigning a returned value to a local variable, then returning it and assigning *that* returned value to a local variable, then returning it and assigning *that* returned value … all you need to remember is that all functions can return values of the declared type. It doesn't matter if they are 'normal' or recursive functions; nor does it matter if the returned values are assigned to local variables. Return values are special.

In C on a desktop PC, return values are generally stored in a register (a data-holding area in the computer processor) to make them available from beyond the scope of the function in which they are declared. If this weren't done then, as soon as you exited a function, the return value would be discarded – which would make it impossible to pass that value back to the code that called the function!

The implementation of return values may be different in different languages and machine architectures. But for our purposes, those details are unimportant. What *is* important is to understand is that a value that is returned must necessarily be accessible from beyond the scope of the function that returns it. So even though the value returned in my code is assigned to a local variable, `total`, that value continues to be accessible (to the code that called the function) after the function exits.

6 – Iteration and Recursion

You can do many calculations using either recursion, iteration or mathematics. So when and why should you use recursion?

Even though recursion is useful, you can often achieve the same results, more easily, without using recursion. The real 'problem' with recursive programs is that they can get quite complicated quite quickly.

Recursion, Iteration and Arithmetic

Recursive operations are often more difficult to understand than operations that rely on iteration or arithmetic. Let's look at an example:

RecursionAndIteration

```
int sum_recursion(int n) {
    int total;

    if (n == 1) {
        total = 1;
    } else {
        total = n + sum_recursion(n - 1);
    }
    return total;
}

int sum_iteration(int n) {
    int total;

    total = 0;
    for (int i = 1; i <= n; i++) {
        total += i;
    }
    return total;
}
```

This starts with our old favourite recursive function, `sum_recursion()`. This is exactly the same function we looked at in the *Recursion3* project but without the code that was added for debugging purposes, (the `printf()` statements, and the `newnum` and `callnum` variables). I've simply passed `n-1` as the argument when the function is called recursively.

In the `sum_iteration()` function I've done the same calculation using iteration. There is no recursion in this function. The code loops through the values sequentially:

```
for (int i = 1; i <= n; i++) {
    total += i;
}
```

For the sake of comparison, I've also done this same calculation using simple arithmetic: `(n * (n+1)) / 2)`. In the `main()` function, I test out these three alternatives. First I call the recursive function, then the iterative function and finally I use arithmetic:

```
int main(int argc, char** argv) {
    int n = 17;
        // recursion
    printf("Sum of the first %d integers using recursion is %d\n", n,
        sum_recursion(n));
        // iteration
    printf("Sum of the first %d integers using iteration is %d\n", n,
        sum_iteration(n));
        // arithmetic
    printf("Sum of the first %d integers using mathematics is %d\n", n,
        (n * (n+1)) / 2);
    return 0;
}
```

When I run this program I can verify that recursion, iteration and arithmetic all produce the same results.

```
Sum of the first 17 integers using recursion is 153
Sum of the first 17 integers using iteration is 153
Sum of the first 17 integers using mathematics is 153
```

Clearly the arithmetical version here is the shortest and simplest way of doing this calculation. If you need to do some calculation that can be expressed mathematically, that may be the best way. Though this only works, of course, when you are working with numbers. As we'll see, recursion can be used for other things too. And, of course, when using mathematics, you need to know – and understand – the mathematical operations required.

If you are operating on a well-defined sequence of values or data items, then iteration may be the best way to deal with the task. The `for` loop in `sum_iteration()` provides a simple way of incrementing a series of values and using them in order to calculate their total. Compare it with the recursive `sum_recursion()` function and I think you'd have to agree that the iterative version is easier to understand.

Recursion is more generally useful when you want to do some more complex operations repeatedly in a way that can't be expressed mathematically and which might require lots of special-case tests if you were to use iteration. If you start by writing iterative code and you find that you have to *repeat* your code frequently, the chances are that the problem might be better handled using recursion.

Recursing Fibonacci Numbers

One of the examples of recursion that crops up occasionally in academic books on computer science is the calculation of a series of Fibonacci numbers.

Many of us go through our entire programming careers without ever finding any practical reason for doing this. Even so, this has become one of the things that authors of books on algorithms seem to think we should all be able to do. So let's do it. If you load up the *Fibonacci1* project you can see how I've written this recursively in C:

Fibonacci1

```
int fibonacci_recursion(int n) {
    int r;

    number_of_calls += 1;
    switch (n) {
    case 0:
        r = 0;
        break;
    case 1:
        r = 1;
        break;
    default:
        r = fibonacci_recursion(n - 1) + fibonacci_recursion(n - 2);
        break;
    }
    return r;
}
```

In fact, look here and you'll see I've made two recursive calls in a single line of code!

```
r = FibonacciRecursion(n-1)+FibonacciRecursion(n-2);
```

What are Fibonacci Numbers?

A Fibonacci sequence is a series of integers in which each integer is the sum of the two integers that preceded it: 1, 1, 2, 3, 5, 8, 13 and so on. From our previous programs you should see that a sequence, generated by repetitive arithmetical operations, seems a good candidate for recursion.

Let's see what the *Fibonacci1* program does. It makes two special cases. First, if the input value, `n`, which is the index into the Fibonacci sequence, is 0 or 1, then the return value `r` is 0 or 1:

```
case 0:
    r = 0;
    break;
case 1:
    r = 1;
    break;
```

Otherwise, add the previous number in the series (`n - 1`) to the last-but-one number in the series (`n - 2`):

```
default:
    r = fibonacci_recursion(n - 1) + fibonacci_recursion(n - 2);
    break;
```

Don't worry if the double recursive function-call here seems baffling. The important thing to understand is that the logic of calculating the Fibonacci numbers requires the addition of the number at index `n-1` to the number at index `n-2`.

In `main()` I run a loop that calls the `fibonacci_recursion()` function with the numbers 0 to 9 to calculate the number at each of those indexes (the first ten numbers) in the Fibonacci sequence. Here `number_of_calls` is a `long long` integer:

```
for (int i = 0; i < 10; i++) {
    number_of_calls = 0;
    r = fibonacci_recursion(i);
    printf("a) The %d Fibonacci number is %d (with %lld calls)\n", i, r,
        number_of_calls);
}
```

And sure enough it shows the correct results:

```
a) The 0 Fibonacci number is 0 (with 1 calls)
a) The 1 Fibonacci number is 1 (with 1 calls)
a) The 2 Fibonacci number is 1 (with 3 calls)
a) The 3 Fibonacci number is 2 (with 5 calls)
a) The 4 Fibonacci number is 3 (with 9 calls)
a) The 5 Fibonacci number is 5 (with 15 calls)
a) The 6 Fibonacci number is 8 (with 25 calls)
a) The 7 Fibonacci number is 13 (with 41 calls)
a) The 8 Fibonacci number is 21 (with 67 calls)
a) The 9 Fibonacci number is 34 (with 109 calls)
```

But there is a problem. This may not be obvious if you calculate from 0 to 9 in the sequence. It will be much more obvious, though, if you try to calculate higher values. Let's try the 45th number, for example.

```
int r;
r = fibonacci_recursion(45);
```

When I run this code I have plenty of time to go and make myself a cup of coffee while the program labours through the calculation. In fact, at first all I see is a blank command window. It looks as though nothing is happening. But that's not true. A great deal is happening. Far too much, in fact, is happening.

This is due to the fact that, for each number in the series, the number of recursive calls needed to do the calculation grows exponentially. In my program, I print the number of times the function is called. The number of recursive function-calls needed to calculate each new number is the sum of the calls needed to calculate the two previous numbers plus 1. Early in the sequence, the rate of increase seems fairly moderate: 1 call, 3 calls, 5 calls, 9 calls …

But the further we go, the larger the number gets. By the time we get to the 20th number we are making 21,891 calls. The 30th number requires well over 2 million function-calls. As we start calculating beyond that (to 40), the calculation becomes incredibly slow due to the vastly increasing number of function-calls.

By the time we get to the 45th number in the sequence, the `fibonacci_recursion()` function is called 3,672,623,805 times! Once I've made my cup of coffee, I come back to my program and see that this is what it displays:

```
The 45 Fibonacci number is 1134903170 (with 3672623805 calls)
```

No wonder this is so horribly slow!

Iterating Fibonacci Numbers

How does iteration compare with recursion as a way of calculating Fibonacci numbers? The `fibonacci_iteration()` function performs essentially the same calculation as the `fibonacci_recursion()` function using iteration inside a `for` loop rather than recursion:

Fibonacci1

```
int fibonacci_iteration(int n) {
    int r = 1;
    int y = 0;

    switch (n) {
    case 0:
        r = 0;
        break;
    case 1:
        r = 1;
        break;
    default:
        for (int i = 1; i < n; i++) {
            r += y;
            y = r - y;
        }
        break;
    }
    return r;
}
```

With iteration we avoid the problem we ran into with the exponential growth of recursive function-calls. The code of the `fibonacci_iteration()` function simply counts from 1 to `n` and calculates the numbers in a very simple way.

What is Iteration?

In computer programming, iteration describes the process of executing one or more statements a certain number of times. Often we iterate over X number of items or count something X number of times inside a loop. No recursion is required!

Let's see this works with an example. We know that the 4th Fibonacci number (not counting 0) is 3. So let's call this function with 4 to see if it gets the calculation right:

```
r = fibonacci_iteration(4);
```

So, the n parameter would have the value 4:

```
int fibonacci_iteration(int n)
```

That means that this loop iterates from 1 to 3:

```
for (int i = 1; i < n; i++) {
    r += y;
    y = r - y;
}
```

On the 1st turn through the loop:
r is 1 + y which is 0. So: r is 1
y is r - 0; that's 1 - 0. So: y is 1

On the 2nd turn through the loop:
r is 1 + y (which is 1). So: r is 2
y is r - y; that's 2 - 1. So: y is 1

On the 3rd turn through the loop.
r is 2 + y (which is 1). So: r is 3
y is r - y; that's 3 - 1. So: y is 2

The final value for r is 3 because i is now incremented to 4 which is no longer less than n (which is also 4) and thus the function returns 3.

Why is i 4?

In a for loop the counter, i, is incremented *at the end of the loop* which is why i is 4 after the third turn through this loop.

The fibonacci_iteration() function works out other numbers in the same way: 0 to 9 is no problem:

```
for (int i = 0; i < 10; i++) {
    number_of_calls = 0;
    r = fibonacci_iteration(i);
    printf("The %d Fibonacci number is %ld\n", i, r);
}
```

```
The 0 Fibonacci number is 0
The 1 Fibonacci number is 1
The 2 Fibonacci number is 1
The 3 Fibonacci number is 2
The 4 Fibonacci number is 3
The 5 Fibonacci number is 5
The 6 Fibonacci number is 8
The 7 Fibonacci number is 13
The 8 Fibonacci number is 21
The 9 Fibonacci number is 34
```

As for that troublesome 45 which made the recursive calculations almost grind to a halt, well, using iteration this can be done almost instantly:

```
r = fibonacci_iteration(45);
printf("\n\nThe %d Fibonacci number is %ld\n", 45, r);
```

When I run this, the result appears almost immediately, leaving me no time at all to go and make a cup of coffee:

```
The 45 Fibonacci number is 1134903170
```

In this case, iteration turns out to be a much more efficient technique than recursion. This is a good example of why, just because you *can* do something with recursion, that doesn't mean that recursion is always the best technique to use. In the next chapter I'll look at another problem you may experience with recursion – infinite recursion.

7 – Problems and Side Effects

You can get some pretty nasty bugs when using recursion. So it is worth getting to know which are the commonest bugs – and how to avoid them.

Probably the most common – and dangerous – bug that you'll encounter when using recursion is *infinite* recursion. Infinite recursion occurs when there is no well-defined end point to stop recursion. When that happens your code will try to recurse forever.

The end result is that your program will run out of stack space – the memory set aside to handle function-calls – and it will crash. But even if it doesn't crash, a program that recurses forever would be no good to anyone. It would just stuck in a function that carries on doing the same thing time after time, so it would never getting around to running the rest of the code. To avoid this, you must always be absolutely certain that every function is guaranteed to stop calling itself recursively at some point.

Infinite Recursion

You might think that it's easy to spot a function that is capable of causing infinite recursion. For example, consider the *Recursion3* project (the relevant code is shown in a somewhat simplified form below). If I had forgotten to put a test to stop the recursion when `n` equals 1, there would be no end condition and the function would carry on calling itself forever:

Recursion3

```
if (n == 1) {
    total = 1;
} else {
    newnum = n - 1;
    total = n + sum_recursion(callnum, newnum);
}
```

In fact, this code won't run forever even though the logic suggests it should. As mentioned earlier, a function that *tries* to call itself an infinite number of times will cause the computer to run out of stack space and the program will crash. When run in a debugger, an error message should (if you are lucky) tell you the reason for the crash. Let's see what happens if I comment out this bit of code, which sets the 'end condition' in *Recursion3*:

```
/* if (n == 1) {
      total = 1;
   } else */
```

Now, when I run the program, the function recurses for a certain number of times – as expected – but eventually it stops. At that point, when using the Microsoft C compiler in Visual Studio, I see this error message:

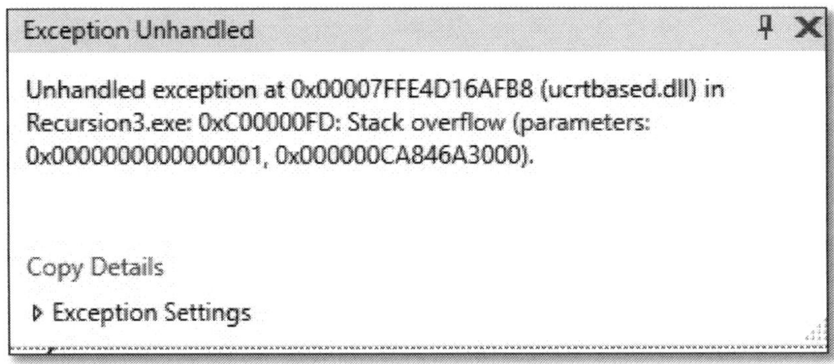

Stack overflow. That is very bad news. If this had been a real bug in a real-world program, I would now have to try to figure out what caused it. In a big program that might not be obvious. I would probably scratch my head for a while, stare at my code and eventually (I hope!) I would see where the problem lies. I forgot to add the 'special case' test `if (n == 1)` to provide a reliable end condition that is guaranteed to stop any more recursive function-calls. I add that test to my code and now all is well. Isn't it?

Well, actually no, it isn't.

That's because my code assumes that the starting value will always be a positive number. But maybe in a real-world program the number will be entered by a user or it may be read from a file. I can't assume *anything* about that number. It is entirely possible that it may be a negative number. Let's try it. In the `main()` function I write this:

```
int startnum = -3;
sum_recursion(0, startnum);
```

And once again, I get the same problem. The program runs out of stack space. That's because the end condition `(n == 1)` is never met. I'll let you think of a better way of dealing with this problem so that this cannot happen.

As a general principle, remember that every recursive function must be guaranteed – completely and reliably *guaranteed* – to exit at some point, no matter what happens when the program is run.

Even if the program is provided with incorrect data (if the user enters a negative number, say, when you are expecting a positive number), your code must test a condition that will cause a clean and correct end to recursion. If there is no guaranteed end condition, at some time a recursive function may try to call itself endlessly. And when that happens, your program will crash.

The order of arguments

Another tricky problem you may come across is when you call a function with a global variable plus a function-call like this (in which `number_of_calls` is a global variable while `fibonacci_recursion(i)` is a function-call .

```
printf("%d number is %d (with %lld calls)\n", i, fibonacci_recursion(i),
number_of_calls);
```

This problem may occur with non-recursive function-calls too but it can be particularly tricky to spot with recursive functions. You may easily be deceived into spending your time trying to fix the recursive logic in the function itself. But as we shall see, that is not where the problem is found.

I've put numerous explanatory comments into the source code of the *Fibonacci2* project (in the downloadable archive) to help you understand exactly what's going on. You may want to take some time to read through those comments too. First, here's a reminder of the correct way to call the `fibonacci_recursion()` function:

Fibonacci2

```
int r;
for (int i = 0; i < 10; i++) {
    number_of_calls = 0;
    r = fibonacci_recursion(i);
    printf("a) The %d Fibonacci number is %d (with %lld calls)\n", i, r,
        number_of_calls);
}
```

This works fine. Here are the results:

```
a) The 0 Fibonacci number is 0 (with 1 calls)
a) The 1 Fibonacci number is 1 (with 1 calls)
a) The 2 Fibonacci number is 1 (with 3 calls)
a) The 3 Fibonacci number is 2 (with 5 calls)
a) The 4 Fibonacci number is 3 (with 9 calls)
a) The 5 Fibonacci number is 5 (with 15 calls)
a) The 6 Fibonacci number is 8 (with 25 calls)
a) The 7 Fibonacci number is 13 (with 41 calls)
a) The 8 Fibonacci number is 21 (with 67 calls)
a) The 9 Fibonacci number is 34 (with 109 calls)
```

But then I think to myself: I really don't need that local variable `r`. I can just display the returned value in the `printf()` statement like this:

```
printf("b) The %d Fibonacci number is %d (with %lld calls)\n", i,
fibonacci_recursion(i), number_of_calls);
```

The Fibonacci numbers are correctly calculated:

```
b) The 0 Fibonacci number is 0 (with 0 calls)
b) The 1 Fibonacci number is 1 (with 0 calls)
b) The 2 Fibonacci number is 1 (with 0 calls)
b) The 3 Fibonacci number is 2 (with 0 calls)
b) The 4 Fibonacci number is 3 (with 0 calls)
b) The 5 Fibonacci number is 5 (with 0 calls)
b) The 6 Fibonacci number is 8 (with 0 calls)
b) The 7 Fibonacci number is 13 (with 0 calls)
b) The 8 Fibonacci number is 21 (with 0 calls)
b) The 9 Fibonacci number is 34 (with 0 calls)
```

But look at the value of the `number_of_calls` variable. In each case, it's `0`. It turns out this occurs because the value of `number_of_calls` is pushed onto the stack *before* the `fibonacci_recursion()` function is called - so it is always zero! Obviously that is incorrect.

A global on the stack?

Even though the `number_of_calls` variable is global, its value is passed as an argument to a function – here `printf()`,which adds a frame to the stack. That stack frame receives the value passed to the function as I've explained in earlier chapters when we looked at parameters (such as the `n` parameter in the *Recursion* project) that are 'local' in functions.

What happens if I rewrite the `printf()` and change the order of the variables and function-call like this?

```
printf("c) The %d Fibonacci number (with %lld calls) is %d \n", i,
number_of_calls, fibonacci_recursion(i));
```

Well, now the results are all correct again. Even so, this it is very bad practice. Anything that relies on the order of parameters being evaluated in a function-call is a) difficult to debug and b) likely to depend on the compiler used. Don't do it.

My original code, in which all variables are evaluated before displaying their value with `printf()` is clear and reliable. So that's the version I'm going to stick with. And I'd suggest you do too.

Unrepeatable Results?

It is quite possible that you won't see the same results (the bugs) I described in this chapter – with, in some cases, zero values shown for the `number_of_calls` variable. Different compilers, operating systems and compiler options may all have an effect on the evaluation of variables and function-calls. In fact, even when using the Microsoft C compiler for Windows in Visual Studio, the precise problem I showed only occurs when building a 32-bit program (x86) rather than a 64-bit program (x64). The moral of the story is that even if your program *seems* to work as expected, it may not always do so. It's much better to avoid the bug before it happens than try to fix it when it does!

Tail Recursion

You may come across the term 'tail recursion' or 'tail call'. A function is said to use tail recursion or a tail call when the last expression in the function is a call to itself.

Compare these two examples. First:

```
int factorial(int n) {
    int r;
    if (n <= 1) r = 1;
    else r = n * factorial(n - 1);
    return r;
}
```

And second:

```
int factorial(int n) {
    return tail_factorial(1, n);
}

int tail_factorial(int m, int n) {
    if (n <= 1) return m;
    return tail_factorial(m * n, n - 1);
}
```

Both do the same job, but the first is just the normal way of doing a recursive call. The second, however, uses a helper function, `tail_factorial`, to ensure that the last expression is a call to itself.

The reason why this is sometimes used is that the compiler will often be able to optimize the code so that a new stack frame is not created. In effect, the compiler converts a recursive call into a `for` loop.

Because tail recursion is more efficient than ordinary recursion – and you don't have to worry about stack exhaustion – you may find it useful in some circumstances, typically list processing. However, you do have to do more work to set it up in the first place and code that uses tail recursion might be harder to understand.

8 – Stack Corruption

Corruption of the stack is one common, and disastrous, bug that may occur when using recursive functions. In this chapter I explain what causes stack corruption and how to avoid it.

Stack corruption occurs when memory required by some piece of data is overwritten by some other piece of data. This is extremely easy to do in C programs. Many other languages offer you more protection from this. In order to understand the problem you need to keep in mind how the stack and stack frames actually work.

Causes of Stack Corruption

Stack corruption typically happens when you don't allocate the right amount of memory to hold some piece of data. This can happen if, for example, you incorrectly cast a data item. But it is probably more common when you are doing something that uses address, pointers or arrays. Let's make use of our old friend the `sum_recursion()` function once again to see an example of this.

I've added a simple version of `sum_recursion()` to the *Bugs* project. It just increments its argument, `n`, from 1 to 3. When it gets to 3 the recursion starts to unwind. The only thing that's different from my earlier version of this function is that I happen to have declared and initialized an array `c[]` of integers. The complete program is shown on the next page.

I don't even use the `c[]` array for anything. I just declare it and initialize it with some integers. The numbers here are not important. They could be anything. The `main()` function calls the `test2()` function which then calls `sum_recursion()`.

And when I run the program, this happens:

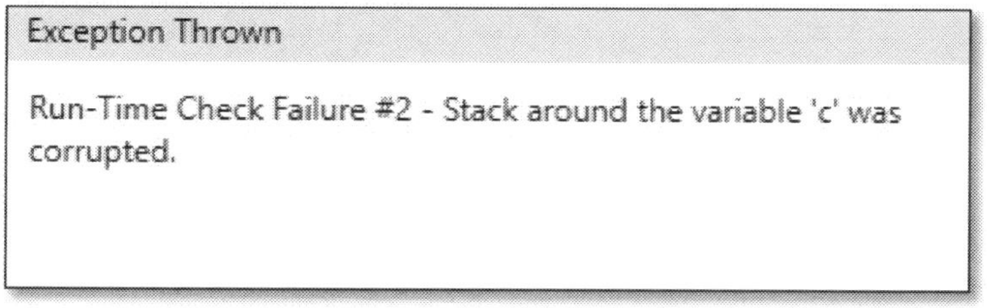

Exception Thrown

Run-Time Check Failure #2 - Stack around the variable 'c' was corrupted.

Bugs

```
#include <stdio.h>

int total = 0;

void sum_recursion(int n) {
    int c[2];

    c[0] = 0x55555555;
    c[1] = 0x55555555;
    c[2] = 0x55555555;
    c[3] = 0x55555555;
    //c[4] = 0x55555555;
    //c[5] = 0x55555555;

    n += 1;
    total += 1;
    printf("n is %d, total is %d\n", n, total);
    if (total < 3) {
        sum_recursion(n);
    }
    printf("...n is %d, total is %d\n", n, total);
}

void test2(int a, int b) {
    int c[2];

    c[0] = 0x55555555;
    c[1] = 0x55555555;
    c[2] = 0x55555555;
    c[3] = 0x55555555;
    c[4] = 0x55555555;
    printf("test1 finished a=%d, b=%d\n", a, b);
}

int test1() {
    printf("At START: total is %d\n", total);
    sum_recursion(0);
    printf("At END: total is %d\n", total);
    return 0;
}

int main(int ac, char **av) {
    test1();
   //test2(1, 2);
    printf("Program ends\n");
    return 0;
}
```

Actually, if I run the program in the debugger, I get cascading error messages warning me about "read access violations" which means that my program is trying to read from some unavailable or non-existent memory location. If I run it outside the debugger, I get a less descriptive error message and my program just crashes.

So what went wrong?

If you look at the code you will see I am here running the `test1()` function which calls the `sum_recursion()` function. Everything starts well enough. It recurses, increments `n` and displays the correct values.

```
At START: total is 0
n is 1, total is 1
n is 2, total is 2
n is 3, total is 3
...n is 3, total is 3
```

It's when the recursion starts to *unwind* that things go wrong. I was expecting it to run the next line of code after each recursive function-call returns:

```
printf("...n is %d, total is %d\n", n, total);
```

And finally, it should go back to the next line in `main()` after the `test1()` function-call:

```
printf("Program ends\n");
```

But it doesn't. All I see when I run it is the first string printed when the recursion starts to unwind (`"...n is 3, total is 3"`) – and then nothing. The program crashes. It has recursed up through the function-calls without any apparent problem but it crashes when it should be coming back down again as the recursion unwinds. It's almost seems as though my program can't find the next bit of code it needs to execute. In fact, that is exactly what is happening as I'll explain shortly.

But first, let's try to find the cause of the problem. I know that the `sum_recursion()` function *used* to work. I've used the exact same code many times before. The only thing that's changed is that I've added this array:

```
int c[2];

c[0] = 0x55555555;
c[1] = 0x55555555;
c[2] = 0x55555555;
c[3] = 0x55555555;
```

If I comment out the array the program works fine. It recurses up through the stack of function-calls, then goes back down again as the recursion unwinds. At each step of the way, it prints some information and, finally, the flow of execution goes back to `main()` and that too prints a message:

```
At START: total is 0
n is 1, total is 1
n is 2, total is 2
n is 3, total is 3
...n is 3, total is 3
...n is 2, total is 3
...n is 1, total is 3
At END: total is 3
Program ends
```

So clearly the array must be the source of the problem. Now in C an array is an address. If you aren't familiar with C, this might be a strange idea to you. An array is a memory location where a series of data items – the array elements – are stored.

When I index into the array and add four numbers, `0x55555555`, I am really placing those numbers into memory, starting at the address of the array, where the first element is stored, that's `c[0]`, and then at positions in memory following that address `c[1]`, `c[2]` and so on. The problem here is that I've declared an array capable of storing two integers:

```
int c[2];
```

But I initialize the array with four integers. C will let you do that. it gives you the freedom to do all sorts of things which may not invariably have the desired effect. If your compiler has range checking options and these are enabled, it may warn you. But if those checks are not enabled, C will assume you know what you are doing and it will let you go ahead and do it.

The question is: *having assigned more integers to the array than the array is capable of holding, where do those extra integers go?*

It turns out that when I add the extra integers to the array, each of them is placed into the next integer-sized chunk of memory – *even if that memory already happens to be in use.* That's because I haven't allocated memory to hold all four integers. I've only allocated memory for two integers (in my declaration of `c`), so the extra integers are written into memory locations *next to* the memory that I did allocate (for an array of two integers).

Writing into Unallocated Memory

Let's look a bit more closely at the problem caused when we write into an array index which has not been allocated for our use. In my program, I create an array capable of storing *two* integers. Each integer takes *four* bytes. So my array has allocated *eight bytes* of memory: four bytes for `c[0]`, four bytes for `c[1]`.

No memory beyond index `c[1]` has been allocated for my array, so if I use the indexes `c[3]` and `c[4]` I will be poking about in memory that has not been reserved for my array and where some other data might already exist:

c[3]	???	???	???	???
c[2]	???	???	???	???
c[1]				
c[0]				

But now I go ahead and write four integers into the array at the indexes 0, 1, 2 and 3, even though I have only allocated memory for two integers.

Here, incidentally, I write the value, `0x55555555`. This is a hexadecimal format integer which is easy to see when using the debugger, but the number itself is unimportant; it could be any integer value.

The consequence of writing data beyond the end of my allocated array is that the memory at indexes `c[3]` and `c[4]` is overwritten with the value `0x55555555` *even though that memory may already be in use*. It may already store some other important data which I have now written all over:

c[3]	??? 0	x??5 5 5	??5 5 5	??5
c[2]	??? 0	x??5 5 5	??5 5 5	??5
c[1]	0	x 5 5 5	5 5 5 5	5
c[0]	0	x 5 5 5	5 5 5 5	5

That memory could have been storing the value of the `n` parameter (for example). Here, it clearly isn't. Because this is what is displayed when the program runs:

```
At START: total is 0
n is 1, total is 1
n is 2, total is 2
n is 3, total is 3
...n is 3, total is 3
```

The value of `n` is displayed correctly. So maybe `n` was stored a little bit further along from the chunk of memory into which my array just wrote? Let's put that to the test. I'll add a couple of more elements to the array at indexes 4 and 5:

```
c[0] = 0x55555555;
c[1] = 0x55555555;
c[2] = 0x55555555;
c[3] = 0x55555555;
c[4] = 0x55555555;
c[5] = 0x55555555;
```

Now, when I run the program, this is what I see:

```
At START: total is 0
n is 1431655766, total is 1
n is 1431655766, total is 2
n is 1431655766, total is 3
...n is 1431655766, total is 3
```

This time, the value of `n` is nonsense. It should be 1, 2 and 3. Instead, it's `1431655766`. That's because my array has corrupted the memory where the value of `n` was stored.

What is that number?

Where does that huge number (`1431655766`) come from? There is a clue here. Use a programmer's calculator, enter the hexadecimal number `55555555` (which is the number I used for each array element). Then I show it in decimal. It is `1431655765`. My code adds 1 to the value of `n` before showing `1431655766`. So you can see that one of the values I tried to add to my array really has written into the memory where the value of `n` was stored.

This explains why the value of `n` has been corrupted. But we still need to solve the problem of why the program doesn't continue running after the function exits.

Stack Corruption May Be Unpredictable

It must be emphasised that the behaviour of a program when stack corruption occurs may be unpredictable. Some programming languages may go to some lengths to prevent stack corruption. C generally gives programmers great freedom – both to do clever coding and to corrupt the stack.

Also, bear in mind that sometimes a program's behaviour may be different depending on whether you compile it in Debug or Release mode. If you compile in Debug mode, the program might work because the debugger may add extra padding – that is, it may set aside some extra memory – to try to avoid memory corruption. Then when you compile in Release mode, which no longer adds those extra protections, the program goes wrong.

In addition, the behaviour may change according to compiler options. Platform, optimization and code-generation options may all change a program's behaviour and they may make stack corruption more or less likely.

The particular C compiler and operating system that you use may also affect the behaviour of a program. In some cases, when *my* program crashes *yours* may not. That doesn't mean that your code doesn't have a bug. It just means that you are overwriting a bit of memory that happens to have less catastrophic effects than the bit of memory I am overwriting. It's still a bug and you need to treat it seriously.

Stack Corruption and Function Returns

Earlier we saw, in the *Bugs* project, that the program stopped running just at the point where we expected the recursion to start unwinding. When the final `sum_recursion()` function-call exited, we expected the execution to return to the code just beyond the function-call. But it didn't. It seemed as though the program couldn't find the next bit of code it needed to run.

Making sense of recursive functions is hard enough even when they haven't got bugs. So to understand this problem, we'll use a simpler, non-recursive example. Because stack corruption may occur with any function-calls, not only recursive ones.

The `test2()` function contains an array which is, once again, assigned more data than it can reliably store. It prints a message and, in principle, it should then exit back to the calling code in `main()` where the message "Program ends" should be displayed:

Bugs

```
void test2(int a, int b) {
    int c[2];

    c[0] = 0x55555555;
    c[1] = 0x55555555;
    c[2] = 0x55555555;
    c[3] = 0x55555555;
    c[4] = 0x55555555;
    printf("test1 finished a=%d, b=%d\n", a, b);
}

int main(int ac, char **av) {
    test2(1, 2);
    printf("Program ends\n");
    return 0;
}
```

There is no recursion. So will there be any problems? This is what I see when I run it:

> **Exception Thrown**
>
> Run-Time Check Failure #2 - Stack around the variable 'c' was corrupted.

That looks familiar. The overflowing array has corrupted memory and the execution never gets back to `main()` so the final message is not displayed. Once again, it seems as though my program has lost track of the place where it should continue once the code of the `test2()` function has finished running.

And indeed it *has* lost track of the place where it should continue. Because a stack frame – the bit of memory that stores the internal state of a function – contains information on the address of the code it should run when the function exits. My overflowing array has overwritten that information so the program no longer knows where to go to when the function exits.

The fact that the non-recursive `test1()` function caused my program to crash shows that stack corruption can occur in any function, not just recursive functions. This is a fairly common problem and, unless you know what you are looking for, it can be harder to track down with recursive functions than with non-recursive ones. To understand this better, we need to take a closer look at how the stack grows.

Unpredictable Crashes

Observant readers may have noticed that I initialized a five-element array in `test2()` rather than a four-element array as in `test1()`. That's because I noticed that the program crash from `test2()` wasn't quite as catastrophic as I had intended since the C runtime showed a dialog that included a button to ignore the error. When I clicked that button, execution resumed in `main()` and the final message was displayed. So the address of the code after the function-call can't have been overwritten. In order to illustrate stack corruption, I want this bug to be as bad as I can possibly make it. That's why I added one more array element. When I did that, the extra array element overwrote the relevant address, causing an even more disastrous crash. This just goes to show that it's not a good idea to second-guess the exact effect of a corrupted stack!

How The Stack Grows

In previous examples, I showed the stack as a structure that grows upwards. That's the usual way to talk about stacks. Because just like a stack of dishes or a stack of cards, we add (or 'push') items onto the top of the stack and also take (or 'pop') items off the top of the stack.

In fact, in many computer architectures the stack grows downwards. So what does that mean – up and down – in terms of computer memory?

What it means that in a stack that grows downwards the address of each frame added to the stack is lower than the address of the frame that went before it. This isn't true of all computer architectures but it is quite common.

I can verify that the stack grows downwards on my PC just by printing the address of a local variable on each recursive call. In the *StackDirection* project, I declare a local `int` variable, `x` in the `sum_recursion()` function. I print the address of `x` (`&x`) both before and after recursion in a `printf()` statement, like this:

```
printf("n is %d, total is %d &x=[%d]\n", n, total, &x);
```

This is code of the *StackDirection* program:

StackDirection

```
#include <stdio.h>

int total = 0;

void sum_recursion(int n) {
    int x = 0;
    int arr[] = { 1, 2, 3 };

    n += 1;
    total += 1;
    printf("n is %d, total is %d &x=[%d]\n", n, total, &x);
    for (int i = 0; i < 3; i++) {
        printf("&arr[%d] is %d\n", i, &arr[i]);
    }
    if (total < 3) {
        sum_recursion(n);
    }
    printf("...n is %d, total is %d &x=[%d]\n", n, total, &x);
}

int main(int argc, char **argv) {
    printf("At START: total is %d\n", total);
    sum_recursion(0);
    printf("At END: total is %d\n", total);
    return 0;
}
```

Here, I print the address of x in decimal format rather than the more traditional hexadecimal to make it easier to see the relative values.

```
At START: total is 0
n is 1, total is 1 &x=[16513904]
&arr[0] is 16513884
&arr[1] is 16513888
&arr[2] is 16513892
n is 2, total is 2 &x=[16513640]
&arr[0] is 16513620
&arr[1] is 16513624
&arr[2] is 16513628
n is 3, total is 3 &x=[16513376]
&arr[0] is 16513356
&arr[1] is 16513360
&arr[2] is 16513364
...n is 3, total is 3 &x=[16513376]
...n is 2, total is 3 &x=[16513640]
...n is 1, total is 3 &x=[16513904]
At END: total is 3
```

On each recursive call, the address of the local variable `x` decreases: `16513904` then `16513640` then `16513376`. That means that each stack frame that's added must be at a *lower* memory location than the previous stack frame.

As the recursion unwinds, and stack frames are taken off the stack, we travel back up in memory to the previous frame in the stack: `16513376`, then `16513640` and finally `16513904`.

But look at the array named `arr`. I've also printed the addresses of its elements from index 0 to index 3. Each subsequent element is *higher* in memory (4 bytes higher as this is an array of 4-byte integers):

```
&arr[0] is 16513884
&arr[1] is 16513888
&arr[2] is 16513892
```

This shows that (on my PC) the stack grows *downward* but an array grows *upward*. Here's a picture to show how my stack grows. The last frame was added to (and, all being well, will later be removed from) the lowest memory area of the stack (even though, by convention, we still refer to this as the *top* of the stack):

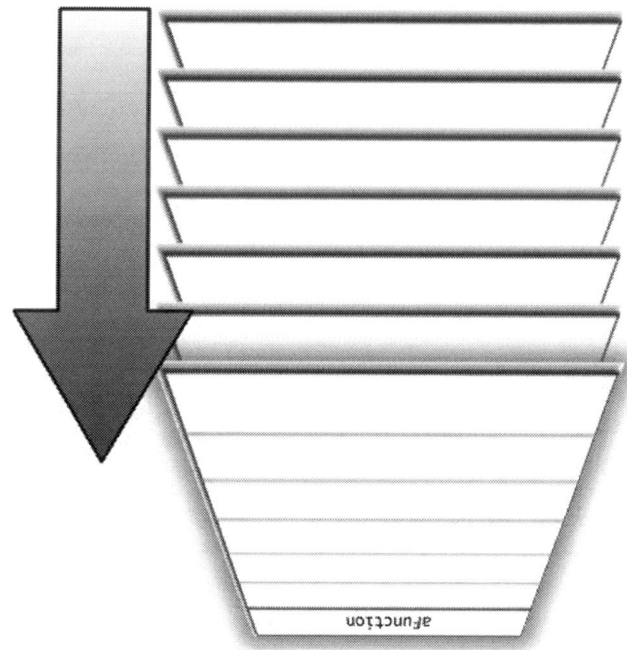

Let's suppose that the function whose state is stored in these stack frames contains an array. As we've seen, on my PC arrays grow upward in memory. The element at index 0 is lower than the element at index 1 and so on. We can represent the array like this:

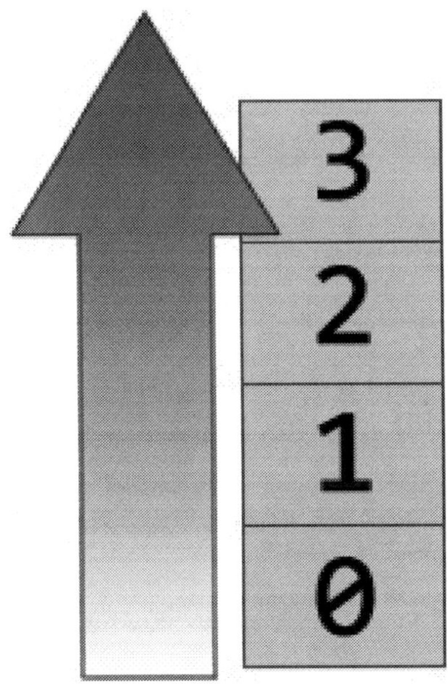

In the *StackDirection* program, I have initialized the array at the time of its declaration. That ensures that enough memory is allocated for all its items:

```
int arr[] = { 1, 2, 3 };
```

But if I hadn't done that – if I'd declared the array and then kept adding elements to it at runtime – the array would continue to grow, getting closer and closer to the address at which local variables, such as x in the *StackDirection* program, are stored.

Eventually, in fact, the array would overwrite the value of x, because the array would overwrite the bit of memory at that address. Worse still, if the array was big enough, it would not only corrupt the *current* stack frame but it would go on writing data further upwards in memory, overwriting *other* frames too: the previous frames in the downward-growing stack.

Imagine the effect of a stack that continues to add frames lower and lower in memory, while an array in each frame continues growing higher and higher in memory. The arrays will poke through into the memory of other frames in the stack.

You would end up with a situation something like this, with the stack growing downward – lower and lower in memory – and each of the arrays in each stack frame growing upwards – higher and higher in memory:

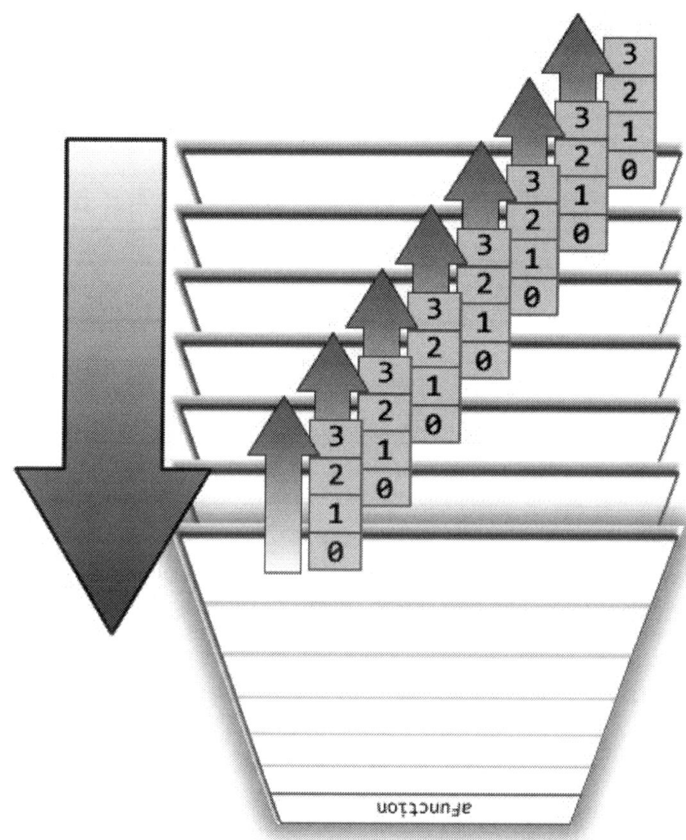

As you can see, if you don't allocate memory correctly for an array – and, in fact, the same problem can arise with data incorrectly allocated using pointers – there is enormous scope for stack corruption.

Stack Frames

I've talked a great deal about stack frames in the book. You should now have a good idea of what they are and how they are pushed onto and popped off the stack. However, this is such an important topic that, before moving on, I will summarise the essential features of stack frames.

A stack frame stores a function's 'state' (data)

A stack frame is a chunk of memory that is set aside to hold the local state of a function-call. The actual amount of memory may vary according to how much data it requires. So if you properly allocate a large array, the amount of memory set aside for the frame will be large enough to hold all the data. If you don't correctly allocate the array, the memory may not be sufficient. As we've seen, that will cause problems.

A stack frame is added to the stack when a function is called

A new stack frame is created whenever you call a function. When a function exits, the stack frame is removed from the stack, so the 'state' of the function, including its local variables and the values of an arguments, is discarded.

A stack frame stores variables and addresses

A stack frame contains a bit more than just the local variables and arguments. Amongst other things, it can also store the address of code that called the function. It needs that so that, when the function exits, program execution can continue at the stored address. However some computer architectures (notably ARM) have a special 'link' register that may be used to store the return address for simple functions.

Incorrect allocation can 'lose' a stored address

The stored address (of the code that called a function) is a bit of data in the stack frame. If something, such an array or an improperly allocated linked list, starts creeping up in memory and overwriting bits of data, that address can be lost. In that case, the program no longer knows where to go in order to continue running after the function exits. And that is why a program is very likely to crash when the stack is corrupted.

The stack pointer and the frame pointer

There is a bit more to stack frames. Outside the function, there are also two important pointers which are stored in registers. A register is a part of the central processing unit that is used for specific very fast operations. These two pointers stored in registers are the stack pointer and the frame pointer.

Frame pointer

The frame pointer stores the starting address of the most recently added stack frame.

Stack pointer

The stack pointer points to the absolute top of the stack.

Pointer Corruption

While you don't need to understand the technical details of how frame and stack pointers work, you do need to understand that once a stack frame has been corrupted, the frame and stack pointers can no longer be relied upon to store sensible, correct and meaningful addresses.

Incidentally, stack corruption is a common way for viruses to infect your PC because a virus may deliberately alter the return address in the stack frame to some other address.

A corrupted stack is always bad. If you encounter this sort of error in your programs, you need to examine carefully any arrays, lists, data casts and pointer operations that you've used and verify that you have always correctly allocated memory for those operations.

9 – Tree Recursion

> Trees are common data structures. They define everything from object oriented class hierarchies to disk directories. Recursion provides an effective way of traversing trees.

Recursion may be useful when you need to move through the elements of some sort of list or collection. But, as we saw in Chapter 6, in a simple linear list, such as an array, it's often easier to iterate from the start to the end – from 0 to the last element. This is not the case with more complex 'branching' list structures.

Recursing Through A Class Library

The class library in an object oriented language is an example of a branching structure. Each class has one or more ancestor classes. If you want to find all the ancestors of a specific class in a 'family tree' of classes, you need to look first for the class's superclass, then for *that* class's superclass, then for that superclass's superclass and so on until you arrive at a point where there are no more superclasses to be found.

Even from that simple description, you can probably tell that recursion would be a good way of handling this problem. I could write a function that returns a superclass and I could keep on calling that function recursively until there are no more superclasses to be found.

I need an object oriented language to try this out. Here I'll use Ruby. I've written the `showFamily()` function that takes a class as an argument. The function prints some information then it calls itself recursively with the superclass of the current class until they are no more classes – that is when `nil` is returned:

class_hierarchy.rb

```
def showFamily( aClass )
  if (aClass != nil) then
    puts( "#{aClass}" )
    puts(" superclass = #{aClass.superclass.inspect}")
    showFamily( aClass.superclass )
  end
end
```

Now I can call the `showFamily()` function with the name of a Ruby class. Let me try this with the `File` class.

```
showFamily( File )
```

This is what is shown:

```
File
 superclass = IO
IO
 superclass = Object
Object
 superclass = BasicObject
BasicObject
 superclass = nil
```

This shows that the `File` class descends from the `IO` class which descends from the `Object` class which descends from the `BasicObject` class. The `BasicObject` class is the root of all Ruby classes and so it has no superclass (it is `nil`) and the recursion ends.

You can try this with other standard Ruby classes by uncommenting these lines in the sample program:

```
# showFamily( String )
# showFamily( Object )
# showFamily( Class )
```

Now I'll define three classes of my own. In Ruby when I want to make one class descend from another class I put a < followed by the ancestor class name after the name of the new class. Here I have created three classes (with no internal data or behaviour, for the sake of simplicity). `MyOtherOtherClass` descends from `MyOtherClass` which descends from `MyClass`:

```
class MyClass
end

class MyOtherClass < MyClass
end

class MyOtherOtherClass < MyOtherClass
end
```

This is how I call the `showFamily()` function:

```
showFamily( MyOtherOtherClass )
```

And this is what is displayed:

```
MyOtherOtherClass
 superclass = MyOtherClass
MyOtherClass
 superclass = MyClass
MyClass
 superclass = Object
Object
 superclass = BasicObject
BasicObject
 superclass = nil
```

So here I have travelled right up the class hierarchy, not only navigating through the classes that I defined in my code but also through their the common ancestors: `Object` and `BasicObject`. As before, I can see that there are no more superclasses beyond that as I arrive at a `nil` value.

A class library is a type of tree structure. In Ruby, `BasicObject` is the base or root class and all other classes descend along numerous different branches. In my example, I start traversing the tree from the end of a branch or 'node' (the name of a class such as `File` or `MyOtherClass`) and backtrack to the root.

But sometimes you may want to go in the other direction: starting from the root and tracing along not just one branch but *all* the branches. That's quite a bit more complicated. Travelling back from a branch to the root involves a single linear search. But travelling from the root to all the branches requires you to traverse a multiple-connected network of nodes and sub-nodes.

Recursing Through Tree Nodes

Another common example of tree structures can be found in the Tree components provided with the visual design tools and libraries of languages such as C#, Java and Delphi. Here I will look at an example using a visual tree component in C#.

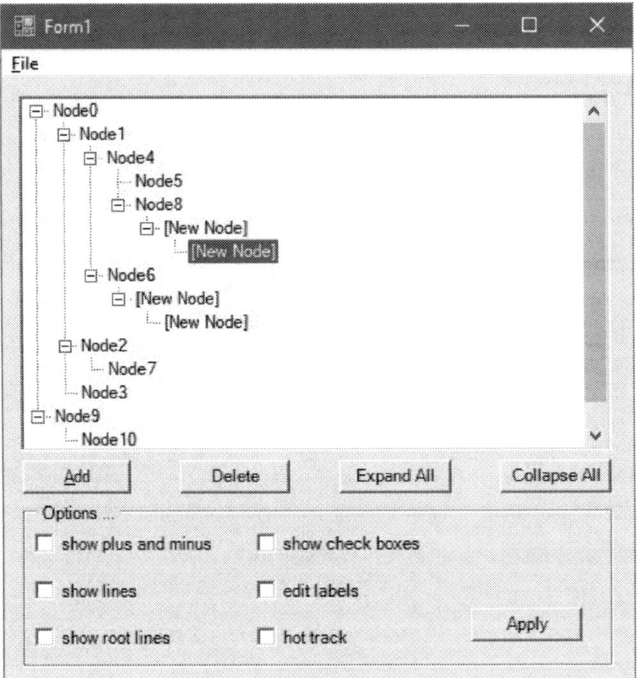

Tree components can be used to display all sorts of branching structures. When using Visual Studio, I can drop a 'ready to use' Tree component into a Windows Forms application. But in order to use that tree effectively – by adding, deleting, counting or moving its nodes – I have to do some programming. Once more, recursion is a vital technique. If you want to run this program, you will need to load the *Tree.sln* solution into Visual Studio. As always, however, it is the programming techniques that are important, not the implementation details of the code that I supply.

In my program, I have created a collapsible outliner with buttons on the form to let me expand or collapse all the nodes (the 'branches'), to add or delete nodes and apply various styling options. The feature I want to look at now is the *Index Tree* menu item.

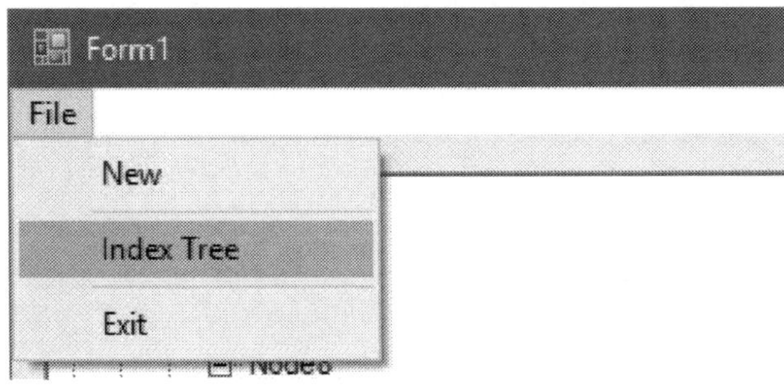

When clicked, this displays information on all the tree nodes. Let's assume it has this arrangement of nodes:

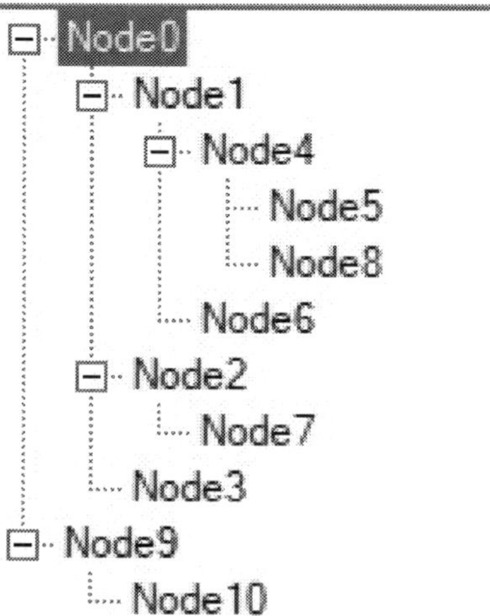

When I click *Index Tree* my code creates a linear list of nodes which it displays in a message box:

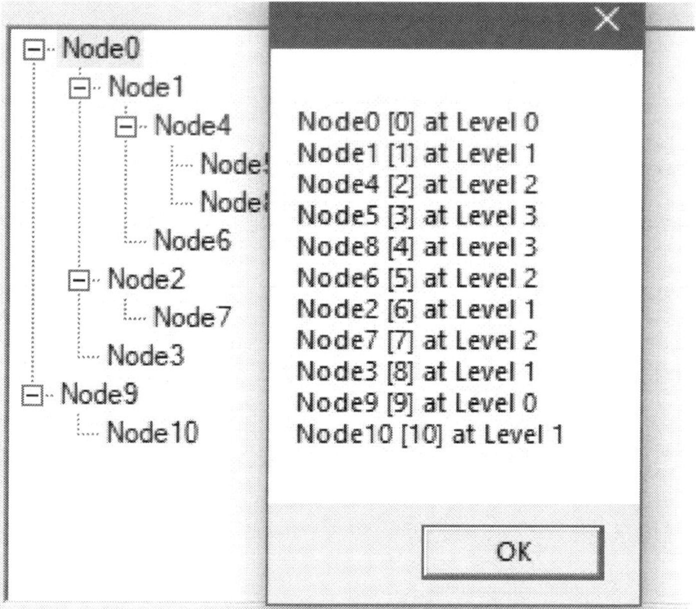

Each node's *position*, shown between square brackets, is counted down from the top: 0, 1, 2, 3, 4, etc. Its *level* is counted as an indentation or branching level from the root. So the root-level is 0, one level of indent is 1 and so on.

Here I have two nodes at root level: `Node0` and `Node9`. These are shown to be at level 0. `Node1` and `Node2` branch directly off the root so they are at level 1, `Node4`, `Node6` and `Node7` are one more level indented so they are at level 2 and so on.

Let's see how my code calculates this. It all begins with the `IndexMI_Click()` function which runs when the *Index Tree* menu item is clicked. This has a `foreach` loop that iterates through all the nodes owned by the `TreeView`:

Tree (C#)

```
private void IndexMI_Click(object sender, System.EventArgs e)
    s = "";
    NodeIndex = 0;
    foreach (TreeNode n in tv.Nodes) {
        TraverseNodes(n, 0);
    }
    MessageBox.Show(s);
}
```

The nodes here – the 'root' nodes – are those at level 0. In my example, these are `Node0` and `Node9`. Each root node is passed as an argument to the `TraverseNodes()` function. That's the one we are interested in:

```
private void TraverseNodes(TreeNode node, int NodeLevel) {
    s += node.Text + " [" + NodeIndex + "] at Level " + NodeLevel + '\n';
    NodeIndex++;
    NodeLevel++;
    foreach (TreeNode tn in node.Nodes) {
        TraverseNodes(tn, NodeLevel);
    }
}
```

This function also has a `foreach` loop. It iterates over the child nodes of the `TreeNode tn`. For `Node0` (in my example) the child nodes would be `Node1` and `Node2`, and these nodes are then passed as arguments to this recursive function-call:

```
TraverseNodes(tn, NodeLevel);
```

In other words, the `TraverseNodes()` function takes a node as an argument. A node may have 0, 1 or more child nodes. Those child nodes are each passed to `TraverseNodes()` and if they also have child nodes, then those nodes are passed back to `TraverseNodes()`.

The result is that the `TraverseNodes()` function can trace through a whole branching structure of nodes and child nodes using recursion. When there are no more child nodes, the recursion starts to unwind.

The `TraverseNodes()` function increments two values with each recursion. `NodeIndex` is declared *outside* the function and so its incremented value remains as the recursion unwinds. `NodeLevel` is incremented *inside* the function and so its value 'unwinds' with the recursion to decrement as well as increment node levels. As always, for a deeper understanding of this, use your debugger to examine, line by line, how the recursion works.

If you aren't a C# programmer or if you don't use a language with access to a visual Tree control, my next example shows you another real world example of recursion through a tree as we look at how to navigate directories and subdirectories on disk.

10 – Disk Recursion

> The directories on a computer's hard disk can be treated as a tree with subdirectories branching off the root directory. Recursion can help us navigate through the directory tree.

The directories and subdirectories (folders and sub-folders) on a computer disk are branching structures. Traversing subdirectories provides, in essence, a similar problem to traversing the branches of the `TreeView` component which I used in the previous chapter.

In this chapter I'll look at two examples of navigating disk directories: one program is written in C, the other is written in Ruby. The C example – the one that I'm going to look at first – is operating system dependent. It only runs on Windows. That's because it uses Windows API functions to get information on files and directories.

However, the recursive techniques work the same way on all operating systems. If you want to write a similar program on Linux or a Mac, you will need to substitute the appropriate functions supplied by those operating systems.

If you are not a C programmer or a Windows user, or if you are not familiar with the Windows API, you may find my Ruby program more convenient to use and easier to understand. In that case, it's perfectly OK to skip this discussion of the C program and go straight onto the next section which explains the Ruby program.

An Example in C

In the *Dir* C project, I start by specifying a directory. Be sure to pick a small one with not too many subdirectories beneath it, otherwise the program will run for a very long time:

Dir [C]

```
GetDir("E:\\Test");
```

I pass the directory path to my `get_dir()` function:

```
int get_dir(char* dirName) {}
```

The code of this function is quite long. You can find a commented listing on page 87. The full code can also be found in the source code archive. The `get_dir()` function appends the 'star' or asterisk to the path name – it's the wildcard character, so that it will match file names when I search in a directory:

```
strncpy(s, dirName, MAX_PATH);
strncat(s, "\\*", MAX_PATH);
```

Then it calls the Windows API function `FindFirstFile()` and it does a bit of error checking to make sure all is well. If an error occurs, the program ends. If all is well, `ffd` is a structure that is initialized with information on the first file found in this directory: `ffd` may be a data file or it may be another directory – that is, a subdirectory of the current directory:

```
h = FindFirstFile(s, &ffd);
if (h == INVALID_HANDLE_VALUE) {
    printf("FindFirstFile failed\n");
    r = GetLastError();
    goto exit;
}
```

Here `exit` is a label that marks the end of the function. We use a `goto` here because when an error occurs we want to jump ship as quickly as possible:

```
exit:
    return r;
```

The Windows API

You don't need to understand all the nitty-gritty details of the API functions used in this C program. The way it uses recursion is what you need to concentrate on. This program navigates through all the subdirectories beneath a specified directory and calculates the total size (that is the sum of the file sizes) of each directory. For help, if you are using Visual Studio, you can select the function name and press `F1`. Alternatively, you can or search for Windows API information at https://docs.microsoft.com.

Now, here is the code we are interested in:

```
do {
  if (ffd.dwFileAttributes & FILE_ATTRIBUTE_DIRECTORY) {
     if (strcmp(ffd.cFileName, ".") != 0 && strcmp(ffd.cFileName, "..") != 0) {
          strncpy(s, dirName, MAX_PATH);
          strncat(s, "\\", MAX_PATH);
          strncat(s, ffd.cFileName, MAX_PATH);
          GetDir(s);
     }
  } else {
    filesize += (long long)ffd.nFileSizeLow +
         ((long long)ffd.nFileSizeHigh << 32);
  }
} while (FindNextFile(h, &ffd) != 0);
```

This starts by checking whether the file represented by `ffd` is a directory:

```
if (ffd.dwFileAttributes & FILE_ATTRIBUTE_DIRECTORY)
```

If it is a directory and its name is one dot – `strcmp(ffd.cFileName, ".")` – then it's the current directory. If it's two dots – `strcmp(ffd.cFileName, "..")` – then it's the parent directory. I'm not interested in those.

I am only looking for subdirectories. If it is a directory that's not a dot or two dots, then I know it must be a subdirectory so I append its name to the existing directory path to build up a full path to this subdirectory:

```
strncpy(s, dirName, MAX_PATH);
strncat(s, "\\", MAX_PATH);
strncat(s, ffd.cFileName, MAX_PATH);
```

I then pass that path, s, back to the `GetDir()` function with this recursive call:

```
GetDir(s);
```

If, however, `ffd` is a regular file – a document of some sort rather than a directory, this `else` section executes to calculate the size of the file and add it to the `filesize` variable:

```
else {
    filesize += (long long)ffd.nFileSizeLow +
        ((long long)ffd.nFileSizeHigh << 32);
}
```

The block of code between `do` and `while` carries on executing – from one file to the next; `ffd` is initialized to subsequent files by this call to `FindNextFile()` until all the files in the current directory are processed:

```
while (FindNextFile(h, &ffd) != 0);
```

So in summary the code which calculates the file sizes in the current directory is pretty straightforward. It just loops through the files one by one, adding the byte count to the `filesize` variable to store a sum of all the bytes of all the document files in the directory.

This next piece of code prints that information and also adds a space for each level of subdirectory so that the eventual display is indented:

```
if (strcmp(ffd.cFileName, ".") != 0 &&
    strcmp(ffd.cFileName, "..") !=
    for (int i = 0; i < indent; i++) {
        printf(" ");
    }
    printf("%s [%lld]\n", dirName, filesize);
}
```

The end result is that this program recurses through all the subdirectories beneath the selected root directory, calculating the total size of all the files in each subdirectory and printing out that information in an indented display like this:

```
E:\Test\Project1\Debug [915776]
     E:\Test\Project1\Project1\Debug\Project1.tlog [9824]
    E:\Test\Project1\Project1\Debug [137169]
   E:\Test\Project1\Project1 [9255]
  E:\Test\Project1 [1438]
E:\Test\Project2\.vs\Project2\v15\ipch\AutoPCH [0]
      E:\Test\Project2\.vs\Project2\v15\ipch [0]
     E:\Test\Project2\.vs\Project2\v15 [1883648]
    E:\Test\Project2\.vs\Project2 [0]
   E:\Test\Project2\.vs [0]
   E:\Test\Project2\Debug [1084568]
     E:\Test\Project2\Project2\Debug\Project2.tlog [4910]
    E:\Test\Project2\Project2\Debug [129709]
   E:\Test\Project2\Project2 [8182]
  E:\Test\Project2 [1438]
```

Now at first sight the code in this program may look quite complicated. But if you look closely you'll see that the complexities are mostly related to the way in which I have to call API functions, build paths through concatenation, trap basic errors and calculate file sizes using information provided by the `WIN32_FIND_DATA struct`, `ffd`.

The recursion itself is no more complicated than in the other examples we've looked at. When we are in a directory, we iterate (we don't recurse) over all the files it contains and initialize a new `ffd struct` for each of them. That's what the loop does:

```
do{
    // code here
while (FindNextFile(h, &ffd) != 0);
```

Here `ffd` may be either a document file or a directory. When `ffd` indicates a subdirectory, we recurse into the `GetDirs()` function to deal with that subdirectory. Then we deal with all the files, and subdirectories, in *that* subdirectory. When there are no more files and directories to be processed, the recursion unwinds.

Here is the complete listing of the *Dir* program in C:

Dir (C)

```
#include <windows.h>
#include <stdio.h>

int indent = 0;

int get_dir(char* dirName) {
    WIN32_FIND_DATA ffd;
    long long filesize;
    char s[MAX_PATH];
    HANDLE h;
    DWORD r;

    indent += 1;     // increment the indent level for printing
    filesize = 0;    // initialize the file size (a 64-bit quantity) to zero

    // append '\*' to the directory name
    strncpy(s, dirName, MAX_PATH);
    strncat(s, "\\*", MAX_PATH);

    // find first file in the directory using a windows API call
    h = FindFirstFile(s, &ffd);
    if (h == INVALID_HANDLE_VALUE) {
        printf("FindFirstFile failed\n");
        r = GetLastError();
        goto exit;
    }
```

Dir (C) […continued]

```
    do {
    // look for a directory by examining the file's attributes
    if (ffd.dwFileAttributes & FILE_ATTRIBUTE_DIRECTORY) {
       if (strcmp(ffd.cFileName, ".") != 0 && strcmp(ffd.cFileName, "..") != 0) {
              strncpy(s, dirName, MAX_PATH);
              strncat(s, "\\", MAX_PATH);
              strncat(s, ffd.cFileName, MAX_PATH);
              get_dir(s);    // get the next level of directory information
            }
        } else {
            // we've got an ordinary file, so add its size to the total
            // note the cast here - the 32-bit ints must be converted
            // to 64-bit ints *before* the left shift
            filesize += (long long)ffd.nFileSizeLow +
                 ((long long)ffd.nFileSizeHigh << 32);
        }
    } while (FindNextFile(h, &ffd) != 0);// loop until 'FindNextFile' returns '0'
    // check that the return value from 'FindNextFile' is what we want
    r = GetLastError();
    if (r != ERROR_NO_MORE_FILES) {
        printf("FindNextFile failed\n");
        goto exit;
    }
    // print out the information
    if (strcmp(ffd.cFileName, ".") != 0 && strcmp(ffd.cFileName, "..") != 0) {
        for (int i = 0; i < indent; i++) {
            printf(" ");
        }
        printf("%s [%lld]\n", dirName, filesize);
    }

    FindClose(h);                 // release the handle
    indent -= 1;

exit:
    return r;
}

int main(int ac, char** av) {
    // get some directory information (note that this prints out the data in an
    // 'upside-down' way
    // if you want a top down listing we will have to do quite a bit more work
    // NOTE: Use an EXISTING Directory name here!!!
    get_dir("E:\\Test");
    return 0;
}
```

An Example in Ruby

Let's see an example of navigating directories on disk in Ruby. The *file_info.rb* program actually displays a bit more information than the C program we just looked at. It shows each directory and subdirectory name, all the files contained in each subdirectory, the size of each file and the total size of each subdirectory. It is also fairly operating system independent because Ruby hides the API from us. If you run it, you will see something like this:

```
E:\Test\Ruby\class_hierarchy.rb : 0K (482 bytes)
E:\Test\Ruby\copy_files.rb : 1K (1119 bytes)
E:\Test\Ruby\file_info.rb : 1K (1692 bytes)
E:\Test\Ruby\recursion.rb : 0K (374 bytes)
E:\Test\Ruby\recursion3.rb : 0K (622 bytes)
<DIR> ---> E:\Test\Ruby contains [4 KB] (4289 bytes)
Size of this directory and subdirectories is 28971976356 bytes, 28292945K,
27629.83MB
```

The `processfiles()` function, is the one that does all the work:

file_info.rb

```
def processfiles( aDir )
  totalbytes = 0
  Dir.foreach( aDir ){
    |f|
    mypath = "#{aDir}\\#{f}"
    s = ""
    if File.directory?(mypath) then
      if f != '.' and f != '..' then
        bytes_in_dir = processfiles(mypath)
        puts( "<DIR> ---> #{mypath} contains      ↵
            [#{bytes_in_dir/1024} KB]             ↵
            (#{bytes_in_dir} bytes)" )
      end
    else
      filesize = File.size(mypath)
      totalbytes += filesize
      puts ( "#{mypath} : #{filesize/1024}K      ↵
            (#{filesize} bytes)" )               ↵
    end
  }
  $dirsize += totalbytes
  return totalbytes
end
```

When the method is first called it is passed the name of a directory in the variable `dirname`:

```
processfiles( dirname )
```

I've already assigned a path to `dirname`:

```
dirname = "E:\\Test"
```

You can assign the name of some directory on your hard disk to this variable, making sure that the directory doesn't contain huge numbers of files and subdirectories (so not the root directory of your disk) as the program would then take a very long time to execute.

Once again, this all starts with iteration rather than recursion because I use the `foreach()` method of the `Dir` class, to find all the files in the current directory and pass each file, `f`, one at a time, to be handled by the code in a block between curly brackets:

```
Dir.foreach( aDir ){
  |f|
    # more code here
}
```

If `f` is a directory and is not the current one (`'.'`) or its parent directory (`'..'`) then I pass the full path of the directory back to the `processfiles()` function:

```
if f != '.' and f != '..' then
  bytes_in_dir = processfiles(mypath)
```

If `f` is not a directory, but just an ordinary data file, I find its size in bytes with `File.size()` and assign this to the variable, `filesize`:

```
filesize = File.size(mypath)
```

As each successive file, `f`, is processed by the block of code, its size is calculated and this value is added to the variable, `totalbytes`:

```
totalbytes += filesize
```

Once every file in the current directory has been passed into the block, `totalbytes` will be equal to the total size of all the files in the directory. I need to calculate the bytes in all the subdirectories too. Due to the fact that the `processfiles()` function is recursive, this is done automatically.

Remember that when the code between curly brackets in the `processfiles()` method determines that the current file, `f`, is a directory it passes this directory name in a recursive call `processfiles()`.

Let's imagine that we first call `processfiles()` with the *C:\test* directory. At some point the variable, `f`, is assigned the name of one of its subdirectories – say *C:\test\dir_a*. Now this subdirectory is passed back to `processfiles()`. No further directories are found in *C:\test\dir_a* so `processfiles()` simply calculates the sizes of all the files in this subdirectory.

When it finishes calculating these files, `processfiles()` returns the number of bytes in the current directory, `totalbytes`, to whichever bit of code called the method in the first place:

```
return totalbytes
```

In this case, it was a bit of code inside `processfiles()` which recursively called `processfiles()`:

```
bytes_in_dir = processfiles(mypath)
```

When `processfiles()` finishes processing the files in the subdirectory, *C:\test\dir_a*, it returns the total size of all the files found and this is assigned to the `bytes_in_dir` variable. The `processfiles()` function now carries on where it left off (that is, it continues from the point immediately after which it called itself to deal with the subdirectory) by processing the files in the original directory, *C:\test*.

No matter how many levels of subdirectories this method encounters, the fact that it calls itself whenever it finds a subdirectory ensures that it automatically travels down every directory pathway it finds, calculating the total bytes in each. The global variable `$dirsize` keeps a sum of all the bytes.

Incidentally, while a byte may be a convenient unit of measurement for very small files, it is generally better to describe larger files in kilobyte sizes. To change bytes to kilobytes you need to divide by 1024. That's what I've done here:

```
puts("#{mypath} : #{filesize/1024}K (#{filesize} bytes)")
```

The last line of code in my program does some calculations and displays the results in a formatted string, using Ruby's `printf()` method:

```
printf("Size of this directory and subdirectories is #{$dirsize} bytes,
#{$dirsize/1024}K, %0.02fMB", "#{$dirsize/1048576.0}" )
```

As I mentioned earlier, while I wrote this program on Windows, it will also run (with very minor changes) on other operating systems. The main thing you need to do is change the directory names and use the appropriate path syntax and separators for your operating system.

Once you've written code to navigate a tree of directories recursively, you can develop it for all kinds of different tasks. You could find files by name or by extension. You could delete all files with specific extension such as *.bak* or you could even copy files to new locations to create backups. All of the hard work is done by recursion.

And Finally ...

Having completed this book, you should now have a solid understanding of how recursion works. You should understand stack frames and the way the stack grows when you call functions. You should understand some of the problems that recursive programs may run into – including stack corruption and infinite recursion.

Most of the programs supplied with this book are written either in C or Ruby. Bearing in mind how dissimilar these two languages are, you should note that recursive functions work is the same way in both languages. This is important to understand. While the syntactic details of recursion vary from one language to another, the technique of recursion does not. It has been the aim of this book to explain how recursion works in a broad sense – so that you can apply recursive techniques, when required, in whichever programming language you happen to be using.

Even now, there may be some aspects of recursion that you are unsure about. That is not surprising because recursion can be quite a difficult idea to get to grips with at first. To get a deeper understanding of recursion, use a debugger to step through my sample programs (as explained in Chapter 3) – and also, try writing your own recursive programs. For example, you could try writing a simple disk management tool based on the examples in Chapter 10.

Good luck – and good programming!

Appendix

Using the Source Code

The source code of all the projects described in this book can be downloaded from the Bitwise Books web site:

http://www.bitwisebooks.com

The code is provided in a Zip archive and you will need to unzip the archive in order to extract the code into directories on your disk. The C code is supplied as single Visual Studio Solution which, on Windows, can be loaded directly into Microsoft Visual Studio. If you haven't got a copy of Visual Studio, you can download a free copy here:

https://visualstudio.microsoft.com/vs/community/

If you are using some other C programming editor or IDE, you will need to create a project in the usual way and either load the supplied C source code files into the project or simply copy and paste the code into your main C file.

In most cases, the C code should compile without errors when using any standard C compiler on Windows, Mac or Linux. In some cases, as we have used some 'old' C functions, you may see warnings or you may need to set options to permit the use of functions which your compiler considers to be 'unsafe'. We have used these functions for reasons of compatibility (newer and 'safer' functions may not be supported by all compilers). In your own projects you would probably prefer to use whichever functions are recommended by your compiler. For the purposes of this book, this is not an important consideration, however.

The C# *Tree* project can also be loaded into Visual Studio. The Ruby projects are supplied as individual code files (ending with '*.rb*'). These can be loaded into a Ruby programming editor and run from the command prompt using a Ruby interpreter.

C IDEs and Editors

If you want to view, edit and run the C source code examples from this book, you will a C compiler and a C editor or IDE (Integrated Development Environment). Many C IDEs come bundled with a C compiler and various other tools needed for C programming. On Windows, we strongly recommend using Microsoft Visual Studio. Here is a brief list of some popular C editors and IDEs:

Microsoft Visual Studio

https://visualstudio.microsoft.com/vs/community/

C++Builder

https://www.embarcadero.com/products/cbuilder/starter

CodeLite

http://codelite.org/

Code::Blocks

http://www.codeblocks.org/

Running C Programs

All the examples in the source code archive are supplied as a Visual Studio multi-project solutions, *Recursion.sln* for C and *Tree.sln* for C#, which can be loaded into Visual Studio. If you are using some other C programming editor or IDE (and C compiler), you will need to create a project in the usual way and either load the supplied C source code files into the project or simply copy and paste the code into your main C file.

Ruby Editors and IDEs

There are numerous editors capable of displaying and editing Ruby code. If you are not already a Ruby programmer, I would suggest that you choose one of the relatively simple text editors such as Komodo Edit, NotePad++, SciTE or Visual Studio Code. Here are a few free Ruby IDEs:

Komodo Edit

http://komodoide.com/komodo-edit/

NotePad++

https://notepad-plus-plus.org/

SciTE

http://www.scintilla.org/SciTE.html

Visual Studio Code

https://code.visualstudio.com/

Visual Studio Code requires add-in Ruby support:

https://marketplace.visualstudio.com/items?itemName=rebornix.Ruby

C Documentation

There are innumerable web sites that contain information and tutorials about the C language. Here are some useful learning resources.

Microsoft C Runtime Library Reference

https://docs.microsoft.com/en-us/cpp/c-runtime-library/

Tutorialspoint C Standard Library Reference

http://www.tutorialspoint.com/c_standard_library/stdlib_h.htm

The Little Book Of C

This is a short and simple guide to C programming by the author of this book (Huw Collingbourne). *The Little Book Of C* is available from Amazon.

Installing Ruby

Installing Ruby

If you haven't already done so, you will need to install Ruby on your computer. Some versions of Linux and macOS already have a Ruby interpreter installed. You can download the latest version of Ruby from www.ruby-lang.org. Be sure to download the binaries (not merely the source code). For Windows users, the easiest way to set up Ruby on your system is by using the Ruby Installer for Windows available from:

http://rubyinstaller.org/

Ensure Ruby is on the 'search path'

If you want to be able to run the Ruby interpreter from any directory, you will need to ensure that it is on the 'search path'. Ruby installers may offer an option to add the Ruby interpreter to the path. You should accept that option when installing Ruby.

Running Ruby Programs

It is often useful to keep a Command window or Terminal open in the source directory containing your Ruby program files. Assuming that the Ruby interpreter is correctly pathed on your system, you will then be able to run programs by entering *ruby <program name>* like this, which is the command to run a program named *helloworld.rb*:

```
ruby helloworld.rb
```

Running Ruby From Windows Command Prompt

On Windows, you need to open a Command window. Click the *Start* menu. In the *Run* or *Search* text entry field enter:

```
cmd
```

This should open a text-mode window. You can now change to the directory containing the Ruby program you wish to run. To change directory enter `cd` followed by the directory name. For example:

```
cd C:\myrubyprograms
```

Running Ruby From macOS Terminal

On a Mac, you need to open a 'Terminal' window. Double-click your hard-drive (e.g. *Macintosh HD*). Open the *Applications* folder. Then open the *Utilities* folder. Double-click the *Terminal* icon. This will open a window into which you can enter commands to run Ruby. To change directory enter `cd` followed by the directory name. For example:

```
cd /myrubyprograms
```

Ruby Documentation

The definitive documentation on the Ruby class library (the API) can be found on the Ruby-Doc web site. Bookmark this in your browser. You should always refer to the latest API documentation to understand the features and behaviour of the standard Ruby classes and methods. Ruby-Doc also has links to other useful sources of Ruby information:

https://ruby-doc.com/

The author of this book (Huw Collingbourne) is also the author of two books on Ruby programming – *The Little Book Of Ruby* (Bitwise Books) and the more in-depth *Book Of Ruby* (No Starch Press).

C# IDE

In order to run the C# sample project, you will need Visual Studio on Windows. It is not vital to run this project – it is only supplied as a demonstration of how to use recursion to navigate through the nodes of a 'tree' or 'outline' structure. If you do not use Visual Studio or Windows, you may want to try implementing a similar recursive function to navigate through a tree using some other language that has access to a similar tree component such as Java or Delphi (Object Pascal).

Little Books Of …

The Little Book Of Recursion is one of a series of '*Little Books Of …*' for programmers. In each *Little Book* we aim to give you *just the stuff you really need* to get straight to the heart of the matter without all the fluff and padding.

We know that there is plenty of information online about standard code libraries, so we don't fill the pages of these books by duplicating that information. Instead, we aim to explain the really important details that you need to gain a solid understanding of each subject and start hands-on programming as quickly as possible.

Other '*Little Books Of …*' are:

The Little Book of Pointers
An in-depth guide to pointers in C:

- Indirection
- Pointer arithmetic
- Data Alignment
- Linked Lists (single/double)
- Stacks & Queues
- Function Pointers
- Common Pointer Problems

The Little Book of C
A beginners guide to the C language:

- Fundamentals of C
- Variable & Types
- Operators & Tests
- Functions & Arguments
- Arrays & Strings
- User-Defined Types
- Pointers

Bitwise Books

Free Downloads

You can download useful free resources including PDF documentation on a variety of programming topics from the Bitwise Books web site:

http://www.bitwisebooks.com

Made in the USA
Middletown, DE
15 July 2019